Modern Rhythmic Notation

MODERN
RHYTHMIC NOTATION

Gardner Read

Indiana University Press
Bloomington & London

Manufactured in the United States of America

Library of Congress Cataloging in Publication Data
Read, Gardner, 1913–
Modern rhythmic notation.
Bibliography: p.
Includes index.
1. Musical notation.   2. Musical meter and rhythm.
I. Title.
MT35.R253M6   781.6'2   77-9860
ISBN 0-253-33867-0   1 2 3 4 5 82 81 80 79 78

Contents

Preface

The accurate notation of complex rhythm has always been one of the composer's most pressing problems—indeed, it is one of the most perplexing of all compositional procedures. Certain principles and rules, formulated during past centuries by consensus of opinion and practice, propose to clarify basic rhythmic structure and to make any notated deviations from rhythmic norms both intelligible and readily comprehensible. Not always, however, have composers and theorists thoroughly understood those principles and not always have they followed the basic rules of visual rhythmic delineation. Moreover, their written solutions of certain rhythmic problems have not invariably provided mathematically precise and visually unequivocal answers to the complex rhythmic questions posed.

Universal, if not uniform, understanding of correct rhythmic notation would seem to be as elusive today as during any period of the past. To compound the current difficulties, the quite recent emergence of "time-notation" concepts has added further problems with which the composer must now cope. In addition to having to determine the proper written forms of conventionally notated rhythmic complexities, the contemporary composer must also deal with analogical systems of notation in which scientifically measurable time relationships are superseded by temporal ambiguities and the intentional discongruity of the rhythmic structure of music.

Composers of our time are thus confronted with a dilemma: on the one hand, their notation is required to be precise and unequivocal if they utilize the traditional notational system; on the other hand, if they pursue the technical concepts and methods of aleatory music their notation must reject both precision and clarity in favor of purposeful ambiguity and temporal approximation. Although modern proportional notation has not displaced the traditional system (nor is it likely to do so, at least in the foreseeable future), contemporary composers must be equally adept within the boundaries of either conceptual technique. As their expressive requirements dictate, they must be capable of making dexterous use of both methodologies, even combining them in one work consecutively or simultaneously. Rhythmic precision and inexactitude thus frequently coexist in the avant-garde and experimental music of today, just as elements of tonality and atonality (or pantonality) often appear concurrently in that same music.

Non-avant-garde compositions frequently exhibit a similar combinatorial approach to rhythm and meter, as well as to tonality and atonality. Igor Stravinsky's *Agon*, for instance, is partially neoclassic, hence pandiatonic in some of its harmonic and tonal language; it is also partly dodecaphonic, hence operational within the special requirements of serialized atonality. *Agon* also freely and skillfully amalgamates traditional and unusual rhythmic and metrical elements, but with no weakening of stylistic conviction.

Musical style, quite obviously, does not by itself determine the degree of any composer's application of the technical parameters, in particular meter and rhythm. Yet the contemporary composer is probably more aware of the possibilities of hypercomplex rhythm and unusual metrical formats than of any other compositional factor except timbre.

Although the notation of rhythm is primarily designed for the eye, it must also assist the ear by clearly delineating organized duration and all interior subdivisions of temporality. In unmetered music rhythmic notation must indicate durational relativity, whether the time continuum desired is mathematically precise or only approximate.

Musical expression in the twentieth century has elevated the rhythmic parameter to primacy. For that reason, if for no other, the many variants of contemporary rhythmic notation, standard and experimental alike, frequently demand explanation and interpretation—sometimes even a basic justification. The several sections that constitute this book attempt to clarify and interpret those variants that specifically affect syncopation, simple rhythmic figures, new time-signature formats, irrational rhythmic groupings within regular and irregular meters, experimental metrical concepts and techniques, and, finally, polymeters.

In a detailed study of twentieth-century rhythmic practices Howard Smither stated: "The analysis of rhythm in the music of any historical period is one of the most difficult tasks that confront the analyst, and the obstacles presented by rhythm in twentieth-century music often seem insurmountable."[1] All theorists and composers, no less than conductors and performers, can endorse this statement. But if the explication and interpretation to come can shed any light on certain of the current practices affecting the notation of rhythmic and metrical complexities, then perhaps this study itself may achieve a measure of justification.

1. Howard E. Smither, "The Rhythmic Analysis of 20th-Century Music," p.55. (See Bibliography.)

Modern Rhythmic Notation

I

The Rhythmic Parameter:
An Introduction

Music is the best way we have of truly digesting time. And of the
five primary elements of compositional organization—melody, har-
mony, rhythm, timbre, and form—it is rhythm that is the most
essential to this function. Rhythm is patterned accentuation and
controlled pulsation, but it is not synonymous with meter. Rhythm is
recurring beat and stress, regular or sporadic, but it is not the same as
tempo. Rhythm is proportion and order in time, but it is not time
itself. It has been succinctly described as ". . . the driving and shaping
force, indeed, the very breath of music."[1]

Musical time, as Igor Stravinsky has reminded us, is both ontological
and psychological.[2] Real, or clock, time is strictly measurable, while
psychological time is variable, being dependent upon the emotional
reactions of the listener and the performer to the music. Psychologically,
rhythm and meter in musical composition produce the effect of
controlled movement within the continuum of time, just as pitch
creates the effect of ordered and relative movement within the continuum of space. Pitch establishes spatial unity while rhythm and meter
confirm temporal organization.

The basis for both time and rhythm is duration. One can experience
duration without correlative time, however, and time can obviously be
perceived without rhythmic organization. Just as duration may be
defined as the substratum on which time is built, so time itself is the
foundation that supports ordered pulsation.

The negation of fundamental rhythm—even the momentary sup-
pression or the calculated camouflaging of inherent rhythmic flow—can
transform a valid compositional idea into an unrecognizable musical

1. Curt Sachs, *Rhythm and Tempo* (New York: W. W. Norton & Co., 1953), p.11.
2. Igor Stravinsky, *The Poetics of Music* (Cambridge: Harvard University Press, 1947), p.32.

3

statement. Consider, for example, the two brief phrases shown in
Ex. 1-1.

Ex. 1-1

a.   Allegro molto e vivace ($\downarrow$. = 108)

b.   Lento ($\downarrow$. = 42)

Here we have two deliberately de-rhythmicized versions of what,
in its original form, is a strong, vital, and rhythmically propulsive
expression of a master composer. Version *a* reduces the pulsation
to a monotonous and undistinguished succession of steady $\downarrow$-note
beats, whereas version *b* cancels out all perceptible pulsation, normal
or otherwise. Thus these two transformations of Beethoven's melodic
idea (Ex. 1-2) are mere rhythmic skeletonizations, the remains of a
thorough draining of the lifeblood of the composer's creative thought.

Ex. 1-2. Ludwig van Beethoven: *Symphony no. 1*, p.41

Allegro molto e vivace ($\downarrow$. = 108)

To be perceived and fully understood, rhythm must be set in a
recognizable frame of reference; hence the validity of meter, which
gives order and stability to rhythmic patterns. Time signatures are the
primary *modus operandi* of rhythmic organization; they establish
measurable, hence easily perceived, patterns of rhythmic order.
Meters and rhythm are often equated, but erroneously, for they are
not identical. Rhythm can exist, even if rather tenuously, without
meter, although time signatures by themselves are meaningless without
a basic rhythm to organize—as witness Ex. 1-1*b*.

Meter ordains the specific recurring and symmetrical division of
rhythm—the number of equal or unequal units of time that a measure
is divided into. Rhythm is the variable division of any one given
measure, a pattern of inner pulsation and stress that may or may not
remain constant. In the music of a Carl Orff the rhythmic patterns are

apt to be predictable; in the works of a Pierre Boulez or an Elliott Carter they are not.

Today's composers are often confronted with nearly insoluble problems of rhythmic delineation, and performers are then called upon to translate whatever solutions are devised. It must be stated, however, that the composers' solutions on paper have usually excelled the accuracy of the translations. In other words, the ingenuity of the creators' notational devisings has not as a rule been matched by the immediate perception and accurate interpretation of those devisings on the part of the performer, no matter how musically and technically advanced his or her endowments. Yet we cannot lay the blame solely on the performer, who is faced all too often with rhythmic complexities that might well baffle even a sophisticated electronic computer.

There is, of course, a world of difference between the motor drive and stabbing rhythms of Bartók, Prokofiev, or Stravinsky and the hair-splitting "paper" rhythms of many an avant-gardist. How many performers, one wonders, could spontaneously and accurately reproduce the two patterns cited in Ex. 1-3,[3] each culled at random from typical avant-garde compositions saturated with rhythmic complexity?

Ex. 1-3

a. Henri Pousseur: *Symphonies à 15 Solistes*, p.14

b. Karlheinz Stockhausen: *Klavierstück IV*, p.11

As fast as possible

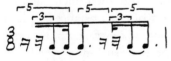

Could even the most advanced musical technicians easily feel and reproduce such rhythms? Approximately, yes; mathematically precisely, no—unless by pure chance. Even when basic patterns of rhythm are uncomplicated, not to say conventional, composers are often ensnared

3. In this, and in most subsequent illustrations, the composer's musical materials have been reduced to the rhythmic structure only, in order to isolate the particular elements being discussed.

by notational involutions. A case in point is the simple triplet figure taken from the second piano sonata of Boulez (Ex. 1-4*a*). As an example of unrealistic notation the quotation was chosen quite arbitrarily; it is meant to draw attention to a notational point and not to a stylistic one.

Ex. 1-4. Pierre Boulez: *2me Sonate pour Piano*, p.15

a.   *b.*   *c.*

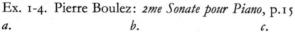

The composer's reasoning for his written format is perfectly clear: he was thinking in terms of three separate melodic voices and so applied the triplet numeral and ancillary bracket to each of the voices. One might question, however, whether the major second, d″ and e″, played by the right-hand thumb in a fairly rapid tempo, could simultaneously yield the two accentual distinctions (∧ and −) that further justify Boulez's notational solution. Practically speaking, the alternative notations given at *b* and *c* would provoke identical performance results, and with far less mental strain for the pianist. The interpretive distinctions between the three versions may well be academic, but the notational simplifications are rather more realistic.

It should be evident that all rhythmic notation requires both simplicity and precision in order best to fulfill its function in the compositional matrix. The modern composer, however, must frequently steer a narrow course between the Scylla of rhythmic hypercomplexity and the Charybdis of oversimplification of a visually delineated rhythmic structure. Ideally, a notator has to strike a delicate balance between conceptual extremes in rhythm and their lucid notational realizations—no easy task under the best of circumstances. It is little wonder, then, that the problems of contemporary rhythmic practice demand such specialized attention and produce such diversified results.

2

Traditional Rhythmic Notation in New Guises

Variants of Syncopation Patterns

As a basic musical and technical concept, rhythmic syncopation is a venerable and venerated compositional device, still indisputably viable in the music being composed in the late twentieth century. And considered solely as a notational exercise, syncopation would seem to present no problems that were not long ago successfully solved by theorists and composers. Yet, paradoxically enough, of all the rhythmic questions to face the composer, one of the most common—and the most conventional in rhythmic terms—concerns the clearest and most effective manner in which to designate displaced beats or time units. How, for instance, does one succinctly yet accurately notate a short accented note followed by a relatively prolonged one? Traditional practice has heretofore favored the notational versions shown under *a* and *b* of Ex. 2-1; more and more composers of the present century, however, have shifted to the formats under *c*.

Ex. 2-1

a.   *b.*   *c.*

Certain other questions concerning the proper notation of syncopated rhythmic figures have not always elicited completely satisfactory solutions. Or, to put it another way, the questions have brought forth multiple answers, one as pragmatic and "correct" as the next. The problem for the composer, then, is a matter of choice, and personal discretion does not easily or quickly lead to standardization of practice.

A cardinal principle of traditional notation tacitly states that the component beats (pulses, or "counters") of a measure within any firmly established meter be as clearly defined from a visual as from an aural standpoint. In other words, primary and secondary stresses that are easily distinguishable to the ear ought to be readily perceivable by the performer reading the composer's notation. This inherent principle makes evident that whatever irregular note durations are present by means of augmenting dots and/or ties, the normal points of accent within the indicated meter are not to be visually obscured.

Although perfectly logical, this principle has nonetheless dictated a rather cumbersome method of combining tied notes and notes bearing supplementary augmentation dots. Certainly notations *a* and *b* of Ex. 2-1 accomplish the objective of showing the normal accentual divisions of the measure. Yet the more rudimentary syncopations expressed under *c* pose no serious problems of comprehension for the performer— even for one far less skilled in reading complex music than an avant-garde specialist. Nor would the displaced beats called for by Béla Bartók and Vinko Globokar, cited in Ex. 2-2, cause undue consternation among most performing musicians today, although both notational forms shown are technically incorrect. Rules may occasionally be side-stepped when the musical results justify a calculated evasion of standard practice, as both Bartók and Globokar were no doubt aware.

Ex. 2-2

a. Béla Bartók: *Divertimento for String Orchestra*, p.20

b. Vinko Globokar: *Accord*, p.19

Throughout the history of Western music we find countless examples of the circumvention, deliberate or inadvertent, of the basic rules of rhythmic notation. If one considers, for example, a commonly employed rhythmic figure that appears in a large body of music from the Baroque period to the present time (Ex. 2-3), simple logic would seem to dictate the clear notation under *a*. Yet even in Bach's time we find this particular pattern frequently written as under *b*. Innumerable contemporary composers have perpetuated this latter version, and some have added a few complications of their own, as exemplified under *c*.

Ex. 2-3

a.   *b.*   *c.*

Further rhythmic notations, culled from various compositions of the twentieth century and listed in Exs. 2-4 and 2-5, represent but a few of the many, and essentially traditional, syncopated patterns written by composers in varying unorthodox ways. Conventional alternatives are given for each figure, not to demonstrate the "wrong" way as opposed to the "right," but to show by comparison the equal clarity and pragmatism of the modern formats. Notations related to meters in simple time are given in Ex. 2-4 and patterns peculiar to meters in compound time in Ex. 2-5.

Ex. 2-4. Simple-time meters.

a. $\frac{2}{4}$ meter, or two consecutive ♩-note beats in $\frac{3}{4}$, $\frac{4}{4}$, etc.

b. $\frac{3}{4}$ meter, or three consecutive ♩-note beats in $\frac{4}{4}$, $\frac{5}{4}$, etc.

Modern format   *Traditional format*

c. $\frac{4}{4}$ meter, or four consecutive ♩-note beats in $\frac{5}{4}$, $\frac{6}{4}$, etc.

Modern format   *Traditional format*

Ex. 2-5. Compound-time meters.

a. $\frac{3}{8}$ meter, or three consecutive ♪-note beats in $\frac{6}{8}$, $\frac{9}{8}$, etc.

Modern format   *Traditional format*

b. $\frac{6}{8}$ meter, or six consecutive ♪-note beats in $\frac{9}{8}$, $\frac{12}{8}$, etc.

Modern format   *Traditional format*

It is not often that one discovers a glaring notational error in a work by a master composer. But in the complete score to Bartók's *The Miraculous Mandarin* the faulty rhythmic notation shown in Ex. 2-6*a* stands out like the proverbial sore thumb. Possibly the error is attributable to the publisher's engraver rather than to a mistake made by the composer; one would assume, however, that either publisher or composer would have detected the error in proof stage. Exs. 2-6*b* and *c* show the correct notational alternatives. Either the value of the short accented note must be changed, as under *b* (and as notated on page 60 of the score), or the ♩ note must be further prolonged by a fourth dot, as under *c*.

Ex. 2-6. Béla Bartók: *The Miraculous Mandarin*, p.59

Composers of the present century have demonstrated a marked preference for doubly, triply, and even quadruply dotted noteheads in various patterns of rhythmic syncopation (as evidenced, for instance, in Ex. 2-6). Primarily a copying expediency, the device is now firmly embedded in present-day notation of certain rhythmic patterns. If all contemporary notational practice were as clear and pragmatic, the performer's task, no less than the composer's, would be made that much easier. And unless completely new systems of note augmentation in metrical music are formulated and widely utilized, conventionally dotted noteheads will continue to express in the clearest manner the syncopated patterns favored by contemporary composers.

Alternative Notations

Like syncopation, other areas of rhythmical delineation frequently suggest several alternative forms for their notation. Musicians often face a choice between two notations of a specific rhythmic figure or extended pattern, both technically correct and both visually clear, yet neither possessing an evident superiority. For example: in $\frac{3}{4}$ (or spanning three ♩ notes in a meter with a larger numerator) one can write either of the notations demonstrated in Ex. 2-7. Both forms are technically accurate and both will produce identical aural results. The second (*b*) is admittedly more concise, having one less note symbol than version *a*, yet *a* more clearly delineates the individual beats, or pulses, of the $\frac{3}{4}$ measure. Preference for the one over the other, therefore, becomes a subjective rather than an objective decision.

Ex. 2-7

a.   *b.*

Modern rhythmic usage is replete with such instances. Frequently the separate versions contain the identical number of note symbols, so that one's choice cannot be influenced by the virtue of conciseness over the drawback of prolixity. In Ex. 2-8, for instance, both notations contain three note symbols. Though the first (*a*) shows more clearly each ♪ note of the $\frac{3}{8}$ meter in operation, the second (*b*) can surely pose no intellectual strain for any musician with even the most casual of training. One's choice of notation, again, is dependent not upon an indisputably demonstrated supremacy but upon a purely subjective rationalization.

Ex. 2-8

a.   *b.*

The figures in Exs. 2-9 and 2-10 represent archetypal rhythmic patterns that may be expressed by more than a single notation; each written form is of equal validity and visual clarity. In the context of a more abstract contemporary expression, the notations in the left-hand column would seem most appropriate; in the context of a more traditional ambience, those in the right-hand column would best serve.

Ex. 2-9. Simple-time meters.

a. $\frac{2}{4}$ meter, or two consecutive ♩-note beats in $\frac{3}{4}$, $\frac{4}{4}$, etc.

Modern format   *Traditional format*

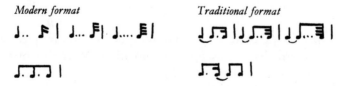

Modern format   *Traditional format*

b. $\frac{3}{4}$ meter, or three consecutive ♩-note beats in $\frac{4}{4}$, $\frac{5}{4}$, etc.

Modern format   *Traditional format*

c. $\frac{4}{4}$ meter, or four consecutive ♩-note beats in $\frac{5}{4}$, $\frac{6}{4}$, etc.

Modern format   *Traditional format*

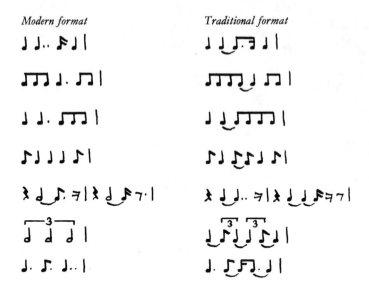

Modern format	Traditional format

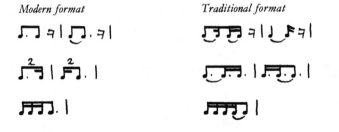

Ex. 2-10. Compound-time meters.

a. $\frac{3}{8}$ meter, or three consecutive ♪-note beats in $\frac{6}{8}$, $\frac{9}{8}$, etc.

Modern format	Traditional format

b. $\frac{6}{8}$ meter, or six consecutive ♪-note beats in $\frac{9}{8}$, $\frac{12}{8}$, etc.

Modern format	Traditional format

A composer, of course, may deliberately choose to circumvent the traditional written format of a more or less conventional rhythmic pattern in order to delineate more clearly such vital expressive elements as phrasing slurs, accent marks, and other articulatory indicators. In *Tombeau* of Boulez, for example, we find certain nonstandard formats of rhythmic notation used to this purpose. The composer's rationale for unconventional rather than conventional beamings is obviously predicated on the principle of articulative clarity (Ex. 2-11).

Ex. 2-11. Pierre Boulez: *Tombeau*

a. p.27

b. p.31

c. p.31

d. p.33

Alternative notations specifically indicated by the composer do not invariably clarify for the performer the intended rhythmic effect. Several passages in the third string quartet of Elliott Carter, as one example, contain rather mild elements of syncopation but are given rather complex alternative notations on small supplementary staves set above the measures in question. In neither instance do the alternative versions markedly elucidate Carter's first notational choice—in fact, they tend to obfuscate his rhythmic intent, especially in Ex. 2-12*b*.

Ex. 2-12. Elliott Carter: *String Quartet no. 3*

a. p.44

alternatively notated:

b. p.58

alternatively notated:

c. p.62

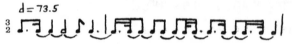

alternatively notated:

On the other hand, Carter earlier in the score furnished his first violinist with an alternative notation that indisputably simplifies the intended polyrhythmic design (Ex. 2-13).

In this same composer's second string quartet (Ex. 2-14), a similarly helpful alternate version of rhythmic complexity supplements the players' parts in several different passages. Many performers will find the implicit polymetric scheme of the original notation more clearly evident in the explicit *ossia* part.

Ex. 2-13. Elliott Carter: *String Quartet no. 3*, p.31

Ex. 2-14. Elliott Carter: *String Quartet no. 2*

a. p.17

b. p.22

It might be argued—and with considerable conviction—that alternative notations are frequently redundant; that if the composer's notation were sufficiently simple and direct to begin with there would be no reason for alternative versions of a rhythmic concept. This is true only up to a point. An experienced composer's initial choice of notation is usually apt for the specific problem at hand. The composer may feel, however, that a performer might better grasp the essence of that problem when it is expressed in a somewhat different visual manner.

Whether the performer does or does not depends, of course, on his or her acumen and experience in solving rhythmic puzzles. Some will be significantly aided by the composer's alternative notations; some will become even more confused by the dual symbologies; and some will grasp the performance solution no matter which version becomes their point of reference. The decision for the composer, therefore, to use or not to use alternative notations for certain rhythmic complexities, remains a subjective one.

New Time-Signature Formats

Although their interest to composers, theorists, and performers may be primarily academic, the formats of meter signatures have been altered in curious ways in many twentieth-century scores. Even when relying on traditional metric and rhythmic concepts and practices, the contemporary composer has frequently employed unconventional written forms or unorthodox placements of mandatory time signatures; these we will illustrate in Exs. 2-15 through 2-20.

Basically there are two prominent variants in signature locale and four varieties of actual meter physiognomy. Within each of these categories there are various minor modifications in both the placement and the visual appearance. One of the most significant alterations of standard format substitutes a notehead for the customary denominator numeral. Visually there is much to recommend the universal adoption of the practice, whether the signatures express simple or compound time. When rapid tempi in compound time are operative, the notehead concept assumes even greater relevance and effectiveness. Certain time signatures cannot really accurately indicate the true fundamental beat in fast compound time: a prestissimo $\frac{9}{8}$, for example, is far better expressed as $3/\mathit{o}\cdot$, and even a moderato $\frac{12}{8}$ makes more visual sense when written as $4/\mathit{o}\cdot$.

Notehead denominators were first used extensively by Carl Orff in his choral-orchestral trilogy comprising *Carmina Burana*, *Catulli Carmina*, and *Trionfo di Afrodite*. Meter numerators ranging from 1 to 12 were related to ♪-note, ♩-note, ♩-note, and ○-note denominators. For his meters in compound time, Orff utilized $2/\mathit{o}\cdot$, $3/\mathit{o}\cdot$, $4/\mathit{o}\cdot$, $2/\mathit{o}\cdot$, $3/\mathit{o}\cdot$, $4/\mathit{o}\cdot$, and $8/\mathit{o}\cdot$ (the last signature representing the top-heavy meter of $\frac{24}{4}$).

Paul Hindemith was also an ardent, though sporadic, advocate of this variant in metrical format, but only when compound time was in

operation. Thus we find such signatures as 2/♩., 3/♩., 4/♩., 5/♩., 2/♩.,
and 3/♩. in a number of his symphonic, chamber, and choral works.

In more recent years, the scores of George Crumb have demonstrated this inventive composer's partiality toward notehead denominators. In addition to using the standard note values (♩ note to ♪ note),
Crumb has frequently utilized the smaller values, including dotted
noteheads, as his meter denominators. In *Night of the Four Moons*, for
example, a 7/♪. signature denotes a conventional $\frac{21}{32}$, while in *Madrigals—
Book II* a signature of 7/♪. becomes the surrogate for $\frac{21}{64}$—a rare instance
of an inordinately large numerator coupled with an extremely short
denominator value. As a distinctive addendum to his impeccable
calligraphy, Crumb encloses the entire meter signature within grace-
fully drawn parentheses (see Ex. 2-18d).

Elliott Carter and Charles Wuorinen have also availed themselves
of notehead denominators, but only when compound durational
groupings were required. Both the numerators and denominators of
Carter's meter signatures are relatively modest: 3/♪. and 4/♪. in the
first string quartet, and 4/♪. and 5/♪. in the *Sonata for Flute, Oboe, Cello
and Harpsichord*. Oddly enough, Carter does not utilize this time-
signature format in such works as the *Double Concerto* or the monumental
Piano Concerto, both of which exhibit the most extreme approach to
rhythmic abstraction.

Wuorinen is likewise content with relatively simple time signatures
containing notehead denominators: 3/♪., 5/♪., and 6/♪. in *Adapting to
the Times*, for example, and 2/♪., 3/♪., and 5/♪. in his piano sonata. In
Bicinium for oboe and piano, however, the composer calls for 10/♪., the
equivalent of $\frac{30}{32}$—a signature that is surely on a par with Crumb's $\frac{21}{64}$.

Perhaps a bit cautiously, David Del Tredici in his orchestral-vocal
Syzygy uses notehead denominators while in compound time but
reverts to standard numeral denominators when his meters represent
simple time. If a composer chooses to use the notehead format in
preference to the conventional figure, he or she certainly should not
hesitate to employ the device consistently throughout a work, whether
the meters are regular or irregular, in simple or in compound time.

The only instance of a doubly dotted notehead serving as a meter
denominator, at least known to this researcher, appears in Stockhausen's *Mixtur*: 1/o··—a durational length of ○·♩, or $\frac{7}{4}$. In this same
work Stockhausen also calls for 1/○♩, which is only an oblique guise
for $\frac{5}{4}$. Similarly camouflaged is the signature 1/○○○; in more traditional

symbology, $\frac{3}{1}$ or $\frac{6}{2}$. But then, Stockhausen has never been known to favor notational pragmatism over visual exoticism.

Whether conventional numerals or noteheads are utilized as meter denominators, some composers prefer to design their time signatures to resemble fractions, using horizontal or slanted slashes to separate numerator from denominator (as in Ex. 2-19). These variant forms, however, are only expressions of calligraphical idiosyncrasy; they do not signify any fundamental alteration of metrical concept. Considered purely as notational mannerisms, the practice is harmless, neither notably helping nor hindering the performer in his perusal of the printed music page.

Exs. 2-15 through 2-20 list six categories of modern time-signature format. It must be admitted that no single format demonstrates a marked superiority over any other. All the variants illustrated are reasonably clear as to intent; all are visually obvious and none offer any obstacles to immediate comprehension.

Ex. 2-15. The signature, whatever its individual form, is placed above the staff rather than centered on it.

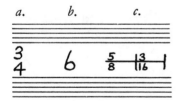

(see also 2-17*c*; 2-18*e,i*; 2-19*e,b*)

Ex. 2-16. The signature is placed between two staves when affecting both.

Ex. 2-17. Only the signature numerator is given, the denominator being implicit by virtue of the measure note values or by metronomic indicia.

Ex. 2-18. The conventional numeral denominator is replaced by a notehead and in some cases moved to the position normally occupied by the numerator (*c* and *i*).

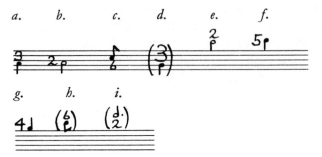

Ex. 2-19. The signature assumes the general format of an arithmetical fraction, whether the denominator is represented by a numeral or a notehead (again, the numerator and denominator positions are reversed at *i*).

Ex. 2-20. An ambiguous symbol substitutes for a standard signature in nonmetrical (*senza misura*) contexts. The last two symbols apply to an unspecified number of ♩-note beats.

A curious—and essentially redundant—aspect of the notation in Joan Panetti's *Cavata* for piano is the consistent use of duplicated time signatures, one on the staff in the normal manner, with numeral denominator, and the other set above the staff, with a notehead denominator (Ex. 2-21). Occasionally the superscript signatures are justified in that they serve to indicate larger rhythmic groupings, combining two or more measures of the meter written on the staff. To clarify further this intent, the composer uses dotted rather than solid barlines within these composite groupings.

The composer continues to duplicate the staff signatures above the staff when no larger rhythmic divisions are indicated, a practice that degenerates into a distracting mannerism. Unless one can find a rather strained logic in absolute consistency of format, there is little convincing justification for such duplication.

Ex. 2-21. Joan Panetti: *Cavata*, p.2

A somewhat milder version of this particular notational idiosyncrasy is present in George Rochberg's *Trio for Violin, Cello and Piano*: all time signatures are placed above the staff but combine conventional numeral and notehead denominators, as shown in Ex. 2-22. Furthermore, the signatures are repeated even when no change of meter takes place. Possibly the composer wished to consider such repetitions as necessary warnings to the performer; they remain, nonetheless, redundancies.

Ex. 2-22. George Rochberg: *Trio for Violin, Cello and Piano*, p.3

Twentieth-century composers have by and large demonstrated a notable preference for unusual and relatively nonstandardized time signatures, a habitude in modern rhythmic practice that will be considered in a later chapter. Suffice it now to say that whether nonstandard or conventional, the meter-signature formats favored by the majority of composers today fit into one or the other of the designs that we have already illustrated. Although it would be exceedingly rash to predict that no new formats of musical meters or of their locales on the printed page will be devised by notators in the future, those now in operation will continue to serve the contemporary composer admirably.

3

The Notation of Irrational
Rhythmic Subdivisions

In Simple Time

In no area of modern musical notation is there greater contention among composer-notators than in the writing of unequal note groups, or "irrational subdivisions."[1] Composers often use inconsistent and conflicting note values when notating duplets against triplets, quadruplets against quintuplets, triplets against septuplets, and similar juxtapositions of unequal groupings. Even within a single work (as shown in the scores cited in Exs. 3-2 through 3-4) the composer may employ two or even three different solutions for the notation of identical rhythmic problems. Confusing and annoying to the conscientious performer, this habit demonstrates little logic on the part of the notator.

There are two principles that affect the proper notation of irrational note groups (identified here as P1 and P2, for convenient reference), and both relate to the written values of the note groupings involved. The most accurate in the mathematical sense and the one most generally applied by composers is as follows: The same note value for both the normal and the irregular group is retained until the notes in the latter exceed twice the written value of the normal group. That is to say, the values in the unequal group do not change until the number of notes contained therein exceeds the number of notes contained in the first subdivision of the basic unit they replace. In simple and in compound time, then, the note values used for artificial rhythmic divisions

---

Chapter 3 is a revised and expanded version of an article that appeared in the *Journal of Music Theory* (see Bibliography).

1. There is likewise disagreement among theorists as to the accuracy and appropriateness of using the term *irrational* to describe irregular rhythms in metrical music. Accurate or not, writers on the theory of contemporary music have used the term more frequently than such alternate terms as *artificial* or *extrametric*.

would be determined by the values of the normal group against which they are set, even when those values are not expressed by actual notes but represent silence. This is the essence of P1.

A relative handful of composers today honor P1 by using identical note values when juxtaposing quintuplets and sextuplets against duplets and quadruplets but go to the next smaller note value when writing septuplets against duplets and quadruplets. Their reasoning, essentially fallacious, is that seven is closer to eight (the first division of four) than it is to four; therefore one should use the same note value that would normally be employed for eight notes as the basic rhythmic unit. Although this reasoning may have a kind of strained logic it is not mathematically sound; furthermore, the great majority of composers do not subscribe to such a violation of P1, to which their notations attest.

Applied to simple duple or quadruple time, P1 states that triplets spanning a ♩-note value are written as ♪'s; quintuplets to septuplets are notated as ♫'s, while all irregular note groups from nine to fifteen are written as ♬'s. To carry this principle to its probable extreme, groups of seventeen to thirty-one would be notated with ♬ notes when juxtaposed against a ♩ note or any of its natural divisions.

Whereas there is a fair degree of consistency in the notation of irrational figures in simple duple and quadruple time, many variants have been used for the writing of duplets, quadruplets, and quintuplets in full measures of simple triple time. These are the most commonly utilized of all the irrational rhythmic groups that are theoretically possible. Taking $\frac{3}{4}$ as metrical archetype, the variants illustrated in Ex. 3-1 are

Ex. 3-1

all to be located in scores from both the late nineteenth century and our own time. Among the seven variant forms shown, that at *d* is the most accurate, even if it is not the most prevalent in contemporary compositions.[2]

The specific citations of notational inconsistencies in Exs. 3-2 through 3-4 will reveal some amazing lapses of reasoning on the part of certain composers, all of them highly experienced and some very eminent indeed. No convincing rationale can be advanced for any composer's utilizing two or more written versions of a single rhythmic idea in identical metrical circumstances, particularly when these occur in a single work—frequently on adjoining pages. Such a practice is not only illogical but is understandably confusing for the performer.

One or two instances cited are actually only apparent inconsistencies; they are included to prove that the eye can sometimes be deceived and what appears to be wrong is in reality quite correct (see 3-2*a*, 3-3*c*, 3-4*b*).

Ex. 3-2. **Duplets, Quadruplets, Octuplets**

a. Béla Bartók: *Bluebeard's Castle*

1. p.26   2. p.109

The quadruplet notation is correct in both instances, even though the total durational spans of the two measures vary by two ♩ notes. (See Ex. 3-25*a*.)

b. Boris Blacher: *Collage für Orchester*; Arnold Schoenberg: *String Quartet, op. 7*; Richard Strauss: *Salomé*

1. pp.14; 42; 13   2. pp.28; 29; 124

There is no mistaking these notational inconsistencies: the quadruplets fill the exact time span, in identical metrical frameworks. Version 1 is the correct one.

2. If the denominator value is increased by half (i.e., $\frac{3}{2}$), the note values of the irrational groups in Ex. 3-1 would be doubled. Were the denominator value decreased by half (i.e., $\frac{3}{8}$), the note values would be halved. The notations illustrated would also apply to three consecutive ♩-note units in $\frac{4}{4}$, $\frac{5}{4}$, $\frac{6}{4}$, and so on.

c. Lukas Foss: *Time Cycle*

1. p.36   2. p.47

A quadruplet in ♪ notes cannot fill the duration of both a ♩. note and a
♩. note. Quadruplet 1 should be in ♪'s, as in the previous examples.

d. Roger Sessions: *String Quartet no. 2*

1. p.36   2. p.37

It is curious that a composer of Sessions' professionalism should use
two versions of a simple duplet in a standard meter and in close
proximity. There can be no argument concerning notation 1, whereas
the second version is conspicuously in error.

Ex. 3-3. **Quintuplets**

a. Jean Barraqué: *au delà du hasard,* p.155

1.   2.

These two versions of an identical irrational figure appear on the same
score page; obviously, both notations should agree, the second being
correctly written.

b. Jean Barraqué: *Séquence*

1. p.5   2. p.11

3. p.51

Here the same composer has used parallel values for quintuplets
spanning two ♩ notes and four ♩ notes; furthermore, he is inconsistent

in his quintuplet values in two different measures of $\frac{2}{4}$. The notations of 2 and 3 are correct, while 1 is not.

c. Béla Bartók: *Bluebeard's Castle*; Charles Ives: *Tone Roads no. 3*

1. pp.7; 5   2. pp.117; 5

Both quintuplets are correctly notated, though it would seem that they are not. In neither meter are there sufficient units to warrant first division note values.

d. Béla Bartók: *First Suite for Orchestra*

1. p.96   2. p.133

This time Bartók was not consistent in his choice of values; version 1 is correct for $\frac{2}{4}$ but 2 is not correct for $\frac{3}{4}$.

e. Béla Bartók: *The Miraculous Mandarin*, p.114

1.   2.

The same inconsistency as in the previous work; here version 2 is the correct one.

f. Boris Blacher: *Collage für Orchester*; Richard Strauss: *Salomé* (Fürstner vocal score)

1. pp.36; 21   2. pp.37; 16

Quintuplet 1 is correctly written, which 2 should duplicate.

g. Pierre Boulez: *Le visage nuptial*

1. p.43   2. p.56

The full measure quintuplet at 2 is accurately notated; that at 1 should be in ♪ notes.

h. Elliott Carter: *Concerto for Orchestra*

1. p.37   2. p.171

Four dotted ♪ notes exactly fill a ¾ measure, but five such notes exceed the durational length by three ♪'s. The notation at 1 is entirely correct.

i. Lukas Foss: *Time Cycle*

1. p.36   2. p.51

These obvious inconsistencies parallel Foss's quadruplet notations, shown at *3-2c.* The first quintuplet should be in ♩ notes, of course.

j. Cristobal Halffter: *Codex I*

1. p.2   2. p.3

Principle 1 is operative even when irrational figures carry over barlines. As the durational span of two ⅜ measures is the same as one ¾ measure, the notation of 1 should be in ♩ notes; version 2 is correct.

k. Iain Hamilton: *Amphion*

1. p.19   2. p.21

3. p.94

The composer has used identical rhythmic values for three different durational lengths; the first and last are correctly written while the second should be in ♪ notes.

l. Bruno Maderna: *Concerto for Oboe*

1. p.4   2. p.5

The first quintuplet should be notated in ♩ notes.

m. Igor Stravinsky: *Petrouchka*, p.114

1.

2.

Comment almost seems superfluous regarding these two notational aberrations, both found on the same score page and both examples within a single measure. How is it possible, one asks, that Stravinsky failed to correct the errors, either in first proofs or in subsequent printings of the score? Now that the composer is no longer with us we may never know the answer to our question.

Ex. 3-4. **Septuplets**

a. Jean Barraqué: *Chant après chant*

1. p.122   2. p.130

Glaring notational inconsistencies in quintuplet figures have already been cited from Barraqué's scores, a failing on the composer's part that carries over to the writing of septuplets in triple meter. Version 1, of course, is wrong; it should duplicate 2.

b. Béla Bartók: *First Suite for Orchestra*

1. p.92   2. p.132

Once again, Bartók's notation is correct in both instances; neither figure requires first-division note values.

c. Pierre Boulez: *Le visage nuptial*

1. p.26   2. p.56

Of the two septuplets shown, only version 1 is correct; that at 2 requires first-division values, not second division.

d. Elliott Carter: *Concerto for Orchestra*

1. p.10   2. p.45

3. p.171

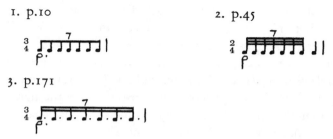

Notation 1 is correct; notation 2 is in accordance with Carter's habitual preference for second-division note values for all septuplets in simple duple time; that at 3 is consistent with his advocacy of dotted septuplet notes in simple triple time. Both latter versions, however, are mathematically incorrect; 2 should be in ♪ notes and 3 in undotted ♩'s, to conform to version 1.

e. Bruno Maderna: *Quartetto per archi*, p.13

1.   2.

Maderna's solution for 1 is correct, but not for 2. The latter septuplet should consist of ♪ notes.

Not a few discrepancies in rhythmic notation concern the relative values used for differing irrational note groups that have identical durations. For instance: in Dane Rudhyar's *Five Stanzas* a $\frac{3}{4}$-measure octuplet is written in *shorter* note values than a full measure nonuplet (Ex. 3-5). In other words, fewer notes occupying the same measure length (*a*) comprise shorter values than more notes taking up the identical durational span (*b*); the composer's choice is not a very logical solution of the rhythmic problem involved.

Ex. 3-5. Dane Rudhyar: *Five Stanzas*, p.26

a.   *b.*

Occasionally composers have substituted a momentary change of meter to accommodate an irrational note group within a prevailing time signature. For example: Alexander Scriabin in his *The Divine Poem* (page 71 of the study score) notated the sporadic appearance of a full measure quadruplet in $\frac{3}{4}$ meter as a $\frac{4}{4}$ measure. And in Maurice Ravel's virtuosic *La Valse* (pages 19 and 22) the composer notates a momentary $\frac{2}{2}$ measure so as to more clearly delineate two ♩-note value septuplets set against a hemiola phrasing (♩. ♩.) of the music's basic $\frac{3}{4}$ meter. Curiously, Ravel did not bother to add the septuplet numeral above the figure, evidently assuming that the ♪-note beamings would show his departure from the measure norm of four ♪'s to each ♩ note.

To the contrary, Charles Ives in his fourth symphony chose to notate an extended series of measure quadruplets in a $\frac{3}{4}$ meter as illustrated in Ex. 3-6, rather than changing the meter for that part to $\frac{6}{8}$. Had he done so, he would have obviated the use of repeated numerals and ancillary brackets, which would have greatly simplified the reading of the part—not at all an undesirable goal for any composer.

Ex. 3-6. Charles Ives: *Symphony no. 4*, p.4

etc.,

better notated as:

Even more puzzling is Milton Babbitt's insistence on notating thirty measures' worth of ♪-note septuplets in $\frac{2}{4}$, with their annoyingly repetitious numerals and brackets, instead of simplifying the visual aspect of the passage by changing the signature of the part in question to $\frac{14}{16}$: 7♪ = ♩. Analysis of the passage, which is drawn from Babbitt's third string quartet, pp.14–17, reveals the following information: of the sixty ♩-note beats present in measures 132 to 161, thirty-three are occupied by ♪-note septuplets in Violin I, twenty-nine in Violin II, thirty-nine in Viola, and twenty-eight in Cello. The remaining beats in each part are filled either by rests or by patterns in $\frac{2}{4}$ that could easily be adapted to an overall meter of $\frac{14}{16}$. In other words, a substantial majority of the patterns in all four parts, individually and collectively, is septuple, not duple or quadruple; therefore a time signature that would more realistically identify the operative time units would be not only more accurate but also more responsive to practical performance requirements.

The *Quintette á la memoire d'Anton Webern* of Henri Pousseur is likewise burdened with many passages consisting of repeated unequal note groups. One such passage extends for twenty-three measures, each consisting of ♪-note quintuplets in $\frac{2}{4}$ meter, with repetitious double figures and horizontal brackets: ⌐ 5:4 ¬ ⌐ 5:4 ¬. One is surely justified in asking: why did the composer not alter the meter to $\frac{10}{18}$ for those instruments affected by the quintuple patterns and thus obviate the distraction of the superfluous numerals and accompanying brackets?

One composer, at least, chose to so favor his performers by translating a protracted series of irrational rhythmic figures into a polymetric passage. Roberto Gerhard in his *Concerto for Orchestra* changed the $\frac{2}{2}$ meter for those parts entrusted with half-measure quintuplets and sextuplets to $\frac{10}{8}$ ($\downarrow\uparrow = \downarrow$) and $\frac{12}{8}$ ($\downarrow\cdot = \downarrow$) respectively.

In another of his scores Gerhard indicated a momentary $\frac{3}{4}$-measure quadruplet in a somewhat curious fashion (Ex. 3-7). The composer's notation is precise in his rhythmic values for this irrational figure; why, then, the term *quasi* attached to the indicated ratio? (See Ex. 3-1*f*,*g* for a simpler quadruplet format.)

Ex. 3-7. Roberto Gerhard: *Symphony no. 3*, p.49

Reference has previously been made to the inconsistent notations of measure quintuplets in Strauss's opera *Salomé* (Ex. 3-2*f*). Additional instances of conflicting notations in the score relate to full-measure quadruplets within a prevailing $\frac{3}{4}$ meter. Expressed by means of momentary time-signature changes (thus creating polymeters), rather than as irrational note groups within a single meter, the citations shown in Ex. 3-8 demonstrate a curious ambivalence on the part of the composer in his choice of denominator values (*a* and *b*). The notation at *c* represents the combination of *a* and *b*, for musical and dramatic reasons that are totally unclear. Notation *b* is especially puzzling as it follows by only a few score pages a true polymetric occurrence in which the barlines of $\frac{4}{4}$ superimposed on $\frac{3}{4}$ do not coincide.

Ex. 3-8. Richard Strauss: *Salomé*

a. p.20   *b.* p.26

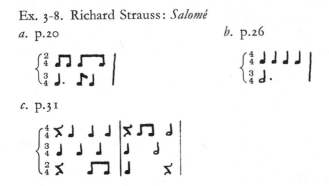

c. p.31

Although not an example of incorrect note values, the brief excerpt from Boulez's flute *Sonatine* merits attention here (Ex. 3-9). The faulty linear spacing in the sequence of noteheads within the irrational figure shown produces an unnecessary reading hazard. To the casual reader it appears as though the ♩ note should precede in time the first quintuplet ♪ note, thus making the measure a $\frac{2}{2}$ rather than a $\frac{2}{4}$. The composer's correct intent is that the ♩ note sounds simultaneously with the first note of the quintuplet, maintaining its full value of two ♪ notes. The fault here is surely that of the engraver rather than of the composer.

Ex. 3-9. Pierre Boulez: *Sonatine pour flûte et piano*, p.13

The preceding examples have demonstrated a variety of formats for indicating the numerical category of irrational figure employed. Most commonly used today, and heartily endorsed by the great majority of composers, is the form that displays dual numerals: ⌐5:4¬, for example. The first figure identifies the total of unequal units in the irrational note group; the second shows the normal number of units that the irrational group displaces. The enclosing brackets are not always mandatory, especially when the note group is linked by a primary ligature, but they do make visually clearer the irregular rhythmic unit, notably when the component notes and/or rests are of varied duration, as in Ex. 3-4e.

Finally, on rare occasions, a composer may have to indicate that a rhythmic figure that appears to be irrational is in fact not so. In Stefan Wolpe's violin sonata, entirely notated without time signatures (though not *senza misura*), one finds many instances of rhythmical situations similar to those illustrated in Ex. 3-10. The three ♪ notes in the second measure of *a* are not triplet values but are required to have a duration proportionately longer than the ♪-note groups preceding them. Wolpe's notational warning is even more essential when the two types of tripartite rhythmic figures are combined simultaneously, as at *b*.

Ex. 3-10. Stefan Wolpe: *Sonata for Violin and Piano*

a. p.6

b. p.7

Irrational values have been applied in recent music to rests as well as to sounding pitches, although the aural result is problematic in every case. The device would seem to work better in theory than in practice, as witness the excerpt from Stockhausen's orchestral *Gruppen* (Ex. 3-11). The temporal distinctions desired by the composer really exist only on paper, precise interpretation by the performers and accurate perception by the listener being physically, if not conceptually, impossible. Each instance in the citation indicates a rapid release of a note from the previous measure by a large number of instruments, each at a minutely different time span within the total beat following the barline. The various irrational figures in the example are listed not as they appear vertically in the score but in order of duration.

Ex. 3-11. Karlheinz Stockhausen: *Gruppen für drei Orchester*

a. p.41
♩ = 107

b. p.130
♩ = 120

c. p.141
♩ = 71

Ex. 3-11—*continued.*

a. p.41   *b.* p.130   *c.* p.141

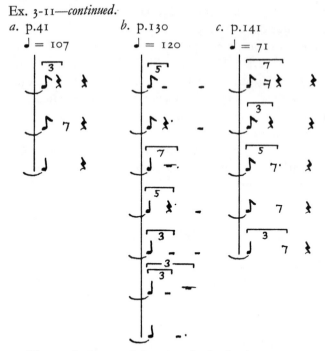

The technique of irrational rhythmic structures is as strongly associated with the experimental premise of current avant-garde composition as it was with certain works of the late nineteenth century— Scriabin's last piano sonatas, for example. Convincing proof of the technique's viability is exemplified in many recent scores of Gyorgy Ligeti and by any number of works to come from Boulez, Berio, Stockhausen, Elliott Carter, George Crumb, and Charles Wuorinen, among others.

The ultimate in reliance on this particular rhythmic methodology is amply and superbly illustrated in two Ligeti scores, *Atmospheres* and *Apparitions*. On page after page in these orchestral sound studies one finds the simultaneous presence of as many different rhythmic figures, regular and irregular alike, as can be delineated in the total number of instruments available to the composer. For example: within only ten measures in *Atmospheres* (between letters H and J), fifty-six separate string voices outline nearly one thousand sequent permutations of three basic rhythmic patterns (Ex. 3-12). Each one of the three figures undergoes 200–280 transformations; figure *a* receives twenty permutations in each of fourteen parts; figure *b*, given to twenty-four parts, also undergoes twenty permutations, while figure *c* in eighteen parts outlines twenty-five different permutations. On any one ♩-note beat within the ten measures surveyed there are fifty-six different rhythmic patterns in operation. The totality, notational as well as aural, is a massive instrumental, homogeneous web of perpetually shifting poly-rhythms. Surely these pages in Ligeti's work qualify as the acme of simultaneous juxtaposition of differing rhythmic cells.

Ex. 3-12. Gyorgy Ligeti: *Atmospheres*, p.12

Apparitions is largely based on the same polyrhythmic premise. Twelve orchestral parts out of a total of forty-six in the measure quoted are written as measure quadruplets in ¾ (*a* of Ex. 3-13); twelve

Ex. 3-13. Gyorgy Ligeti: *Apparitions*, p.20

Ex. 3-13—*continued.*

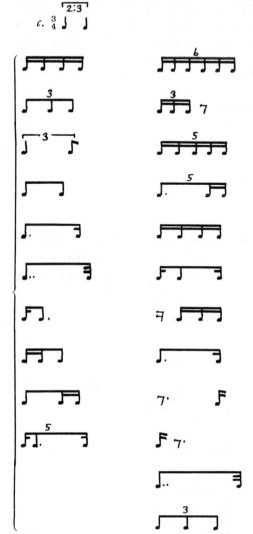

other parts operate within the normal beats of the meter (*b*), while the remaining twenty-two parts are written as measure duplets in the basic meter. The rhythmic figures given under *a* are not on consecutive beats, but merely represent the counterpoints of rhythm outlined on two of the four irrational beats of the measure. The same is true of *c*, the two beats shown being extracted from different measures merely to show the variety of permutations chosen by Ligeti. Allowing for certain duplications of pattern in the forty-six parts, on any one beat there are delineated some twenty-six rhythmic figures. As the passage in question continues for some ten more measures, during which the meters change but the total number of ♩-note beats is equivalent to ten measures of the original $\frac{3}{4}$, one finds the astounding total of well over twelve hundred permutations of the various rhythmic cells. The work is—to put it mildly—an incredible heterophonous orchestral sound-scape, and one that could not possibly exist without the composer's single-minded pursuit of the technique of polyrhythm.

Although its compositional premise is totally different from that which fashioned *Apparitions* and *Atmospheres*, Stockhausen's *Gruppen* exhibits many passages of multirhythms as densely meshed as those of Ligeti's scores. Ex. 3-14 constitutes the rhythmic framework of half a measure, or two ♩-note beats, on the score page cited.

Ex. 3-14. Karlheinz Stockhausen: *Gruppen für drei Orchester*, p.109

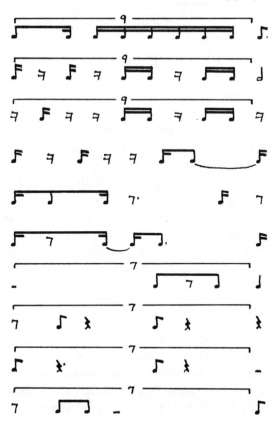

Ex. 3-14—*continued.*

Far simpler on one level than the polyrhythmic premise of both the Ligeti and Stockhausen compositions, yet rather more complex on another level, are the irrational note groupings that form the second section of Henry Cowell's *Rhythmicana* for solo piano (1938). They are simpler in that only two rhythmic strata are ever present, but more complex in the actual constructs pitted one against the other: the irregular figures used by Cowell range successively from 13 over 9, 8, 7, 6, and 5 to 11 over 9, 8, 7, 6, and 4. Each irrational note group fills an entire measure in the constant meter of $\frac{1}{1}$ ($\frac{2}{2}$).

If for no other reason, it is well worth scrutinizing the work to observe the proper vertical alignment of the irregular rhythms so juxtaposed. Cowell also properly notated the values of each rhythmic group and was consistent in his choice of first-division values for all groups from 8 to 13.

One could quote many other contemporary scores that rely heavily on a polyrhythmic technique that elevates irrational subdivisions to a position of primacy. The significance of this approach within the entire spectrum of late twentieth-century music can hardly be overemphasized. Even the most casual glance at the scores of the prominent avant-garde will reveal the extent and importance of this technique. If a ratio could somehow be established between the relative occurrence of regular and irrational rhythmical groupings in all serious music from mid-century to the present day, it would be found that the presence of irregular rhythmic divisions far outweighs the modern composer's reliance on normal rhythmic subdivision. Such a survey would also demonstrate that quite frequently meters themselves have only secondary significance in much of this music, and that barlines have an almost incidental relevance to the rhythmic constructs used.

In Compound Time

If there is frequent disagreement among composers and theorists concerning Principle 1 in simple time, confusion reigns supreme when P1 is carried over to compound time. With the ♩. note as the basic time unit, the potential choices of notation are illustrated in Ex. 3-15. The methods shown are all in current use when duplets and quadruplets are set against the normal three ♪ notes per ♩. unit in ⁶⁄₈ time. The formats illustrated would also obviously apply to any ♩.-note unit within the meters of ⁹⁄₈, ¹²⁄₈, and ¹⁵⁄₈. Version *f* is the simplest, in that it dispenses with cumbersome numerals and ancillary brackets. Moreover, it is mathematically sound, the augmentation dots after each note rounding out the note values required to fill up the total time span of each basic ♩.-note unit.

Alternative *b* is the second most accurate notation, as it employs the same note values for both regular and irregular groups, thus conforming to P1. The quadruplet notations in *c* through *g* show this group written with the next smallest note value (♪'s). This practice is based on the second notational principle with which we are concerned (P2): notes of the same kind always have the same time value. That is to say, if one writes four notes occupying the same duration as two notes, they must be written as first division values. In compound time, however, with its natural subdivisions into three rather than into two, it is not possible to apply P2 in a literal fashion. Composers necessarily must choose between honoring P1 (as at *b*) or P2, as did those notators of *a* and *c* through *g*. Neither choice is entirely correct when isolated from context; the problem, understandably, has confounded many a composer, which accounts in part for the number of variants found in contemporary scores.

Ex. 3-15

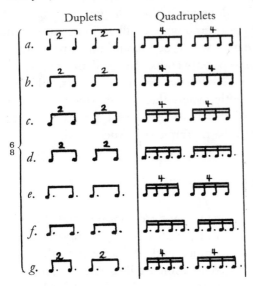

To discover the relative prevalence of the three possible but different notational formats for an identical rhythmic problem—a duplet occupying the time span of a ♩. note in compound time—some two hundred works were examined that employed this rhythmic device. Chosen completely at random, the scores range from late nineteenth century to mid-twentieth century. Of these two hundred compositions, 62 (or 31 percent) favored version *f* of Ex. 3-15; 104 (52 percent) used *b*; while only 34 (17 percent) preferred version *a*. These findings would seem to demonstrate conclusively that more composers agree with P1 than they do with P2 when compound time is operative.

Certain composers, nonetheless, have vacillated between the three potential notations for duplets in compound time, using first one and then another of the formats—often in a single work. A few have even used all three variants at one time or another, as the listing in Ex. 3-16 will demonstrate.

Exs. 3-2 through 3-4 cited some notable examples of indecision in the writing of irrational note groups in simple time; Ex. 3-17 shows further instances of notational inconsistencies applied to irregular figures in compound time. Sometimes the conflicting notations appear within a few measures or score pages of each other—or even within the same measure. Some notations, though they may appear to be contradictory, are correct according to P1 (3-17*b* and *n*, for example).

Ex. 3-16. (The composers' works are coded by number. Refer to the Index of Composers and Works, p.194, to identify the composition cited.)

	𝅘𝅥 𝅘𝅥 = 𝅘𝅥.	𝅘𝅥𝅮𝅘𝅥𝅮 = 𝅘𝅥.	𝅘𝅥𝅮·𝅘𝅥𝅯 = 𝅘𝅥.
S. Barber	6	3, 4, 7	2
B. Bartók	3	10, 12	9, 14
B. Britten		1, 6, 8, 9, 10	3, 4, 5
E. Carter		6, 14	1, 3, 7, 10, 11, 15
C. Chávez		1	3
A. Copland	6	1, 5, 9	
C. Debussy		1, 4, 5, 7, 8	2, 3, 6
R. L. Finney		2, 3	1, 4
R. Harris	2		1
K. A. Hartmann	3	1	
P. Hindemith	6, 9, 11, 15, 16, 17	1, 5	2
J. Ibert		1	2, 3, 4
C. Ives	15	11	3, 9
A. Jolivet	1		3
L. Kirchner		2	1
M. Ravel	2, 4, 6, 9, 10		1, 3, 7
A. Schoenberg		6	4, 7, 10
W. Schuman	2, 3	1	
R. Sessions	3, 4		5
D. Shostakovitch		3	1, 2
I. Stravinsky		3, 6, 7, 12, 13	4, 15
R. Vaughan Williams	5	2, 3, 4, 7, 8, 9, 10	
W. Walton		3	4, 5

Ex. 3-17

a. Jehan Alain: *Trois danses pour orgue*

1. p.17   2. p.19

3. p.20

Of these five irrational note groups, only the septuplet at 2 is correctly written. The duplet and quadruplet at 1 should be in ♪'s, and the quintuplet at 3 in ♩ notes.

b. Jean Barraqué: *Chant après chant*, p.157; George Rochberg: *Trio for Violin, Cello and Piano*, p.23

1. [musical example]   2. [musical example]

Both composers used the correct note values in 1, but not in 2—a full-measure quintuplet—which should utilize ♪'s.[3]

c. Arnold Bax: *Sixth Symphony*

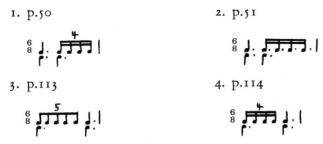

1. p.50   2. p.51

3. p.113   4. p.114

Both pairs of examples are found on sequential pages. The notations of 1 and 2 are seemingly in concordance, but 1 is incorrect, as is 4. The quintuplet is correctly written, producing the curious situation that a figure containing five notes is written with *longer* note values than a group of four notes.

d. Alban Berg: *Wozzeck*, p.59; Maurice Ravel: *Rapsodie espagnole*, pp.52,88

1. [musical example]   2. [musical example]

Berg's momentary lapse is highly puzzling, as the two notations occur not only on the same page but within the same measure; 1, of course should duplicate 2. Ravel's inconsistencies appear in the final movement of the suite.

3. In his *Concerto for Orchestra*, Bartók notated the correct values of both a measure quadruplet and quintuplet in 3/8 meter (page 21):

[musical example] and [musical example].

Sibelius did likewise in *The Swan of Tuonela* (page 3), wherein a quadruplet and a quintuplet covering three ♩ notes of a 9/4 meter are written with the same values:

[musical example] and [musical example].

e. Luciano Berio: *Variazione per Orchestra da Camera,* p.26

1.

2.

The remarks made concerning Bax's work are applicable here as well. Both irrational figures are correctly notated.

f. Pierre Boulez: *Le marteau sans maître*

1. p.38

2. p.38

3. p.40

4. p.40

Although the two measure quintuplets are consistently notated, they utilize the wrong values; they should be ♪'s. The quintuplet at 2 is correct, as is the septuplet at 4.

g. Pierre Boulez: *Le visage nuptial*

1. p.1

2. p.15

Despite an apparent inconsistency in note values, both quadruplets are correctly notated.

h. Benjamin Britten: *Our Hunting Fathers*; Manuel de Falla: *Nights in the Gardens of Spain*; Irving Fine: *Symphony*; Seymour Shifrin: *Satires of Circumstance*; William Walton: *Façade*

1. pp.64;72;96;37;102

2. pp.71;77;96;36;103

Either variant by itself, as used by all five composers, is technically correct, but there is no valid reason for both forms to appear in the same composition.

i. Aaron Copland: *Dance Panels*

1. p.80   2. p.81

The comment made concerning Berg's inconsistent notation is relevant here; 1 is correct and 2 is not.

j. Peter Maxwell Davies: *Antechrist*

1. p.5   2. p.13

3. p.13   4. p.13

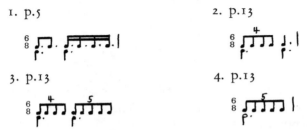

The inconsistencies are visual, not technical; all forms are correct, even quintuplet 4, though Davies might have notated all his quadruplets as at 1.

k. Charles Ives: *Fourth Violin Sonata*

1. p.17   2. p.17   3. p.19

Though Ives's music is almost too full of notational contradictions to warrant special mention, those cited above are typical. Quadruplet 1 is correct; 2 is not. Duplet 3 is correct except that the figure 2 is redundant; ancillary numerals are not required when dotted notes constitute a duplet or quadruplet in compound time.

l. Charles Ives: *Symphony no. 4*

1. p.2   2. p.3

3. p.97

There is no need to belabor the obvious here; the notational incongruities are immediately apparent.

m. Maurice Ravel: *Alborada del gracioso,* p.42

1.   2.

The two variants occur within the same measure—a surprising lapse on the part of a composer who is normally fastidious in all notational matters.

n. Maurice Ravel: *Shéhérazade,* p.9

1.   2.

Again, contradictory formats on a single page of the score; version 1 as used in measure one is correct; the other, appearing in measure two, is not.

o. Roger Sessions: *Symphony no. 3,* p.45

1.   2.

These two notations appear contradictory; actually both are correct, even though quadruplet 1 covers half the time span of quadruplet 2. Sessions would have been more consistent, however, had he written the first group as four ♪. notes, to parallel the format at 2.

p. Jean Sibelius: *Symphony no. 2*

1. p.7   2. p.16

3. p.29

The glaring disagreement between duplets 1 and 3 could have been eliminated by the composer's writing them as pairs of ♩. notes—the quite standard hemiola format. Otherwise, version 1 is correct, as is the quadruplet at 2.

q. Richard Strauss: *Salomé*

1. p.167   2. p.268

A ♩-note duplet cannot fill the durational span of both a ♩. and a ♩. ; version 1, therefore, is incorrect.

r. Igor Stravinsky: *Abraham and Isaac*

1. p.5   2. p.20

Normally, Stravinsky is as precise in his rhythmic notation as is Ravel; it is an unexplained mystery that he allowed two versions of the same irrational figure to appear in this score. That at 2, of course, is the correct one.

s. Ralph Vaughan Williams: *Concerto Accademico*, p.28

1.   2.

Although neither version is incorrect, it is curious that Vaughan Williams used both in such proximity. There appears to be no expressive or articulative reason in the music for this distinction.

Although many composers subscribe to the use of dotted notes for duplet and quadruplet groups in compound meters, few agree on either the logic or the necessity of applying this principle to quintuplets and septuplets. Elliott Carter is apparently the most prominent, if not the sole, composer to advocate this notational procedure. The patent illogicality of dotting each note (or rest symbol) within a quintuplet or septuplet, in either simple or compound time, is not a matter of personal taste and discretion but of simple mathematics. Whereas duplets and quadruplets can, and even should, consist of dotted notes in compound time, all other irrational figures cannot. If the augmentation dot still means what it always has since its invention in the seventeenth century—the increase by one-half of the note value it follows—it cannot be applied to rhythmic figures whose total value would then exceed, or fall short of, the normal number of units within the prevailing pulse or measure. Four ♪· notes exactly fill the durational space of three ♪ notes, but five or seven ♪· notes exceed it. Four ♪·'s accurately fill a $\frac{3}{4}$ measure in simple time but five or seven such values do not. Proof of these contentions is offered in Exs. 3-18 and 3-19, the offending citations drawn from the scores of Elliott Carter.

Ex. 3-18. Elliott Carter: *Double Concerto*, p.53

$$a. \quad = \tfrac{3}{8} + \tfrac{3}{32} \quad \text{or} \quad \tfrac{7}{16} + \tfrac{1}{32}$$

$$b. \quad = \tfrac{5}{16} \left(\tfrac{10}{32}\right) + \tfrac{1}{64}$$

Ex. 3-19. Elliott Carter: *Concerto for Orchestra*, p.171

$$a. \quad = \tfrac{3}{4} + \tfrac{3}{16} \quad \text{or} \quad \tfrac{7}{8} + \tfrac{1}{16}$$

$$b. \quad = \tfrac{5}{8} \left(\tfrac{10}{16}\right) + \tfrac{1}{32}$$

One has no desire to flog dead horses, but this peculiar notational viewpoint, consistently practiced by a composer as eminent as Carter, can be neither justified nor recommended. Perhaps the sophistry of this practice—in visual terms, at least—is best demonstrated by a passage in Carter's third string quartet: two septuplets, one in simple triple time ($\frac{3}{2}$) and the other in compound duple time ($\frac{12}{8}$), are superimposed (Ex. 3-20). The former figure is minus any augmentation dots, while the latter displays such dots after each note. Both note groups occupy the same durational span even though their respective meter denominators differ.

One is reminded of Curt Sachs's summation in his admirable *Rhythm and Tempo*: "Musical notation, it seems, has in all times examples of unnecessary complication under the disguise of alleged simplification."

Ex. 3-20. Elliott Carter: *String Quartet no. 3*, p.27

In certain irregular meters, it must be noted, quintuplet note values *can* each be dotted so as to fill out correctly the durational length of the measure. In $\frac{15}{16}$, for example—a meter that ordinarily would be grouped in three pulsations of five units each, or in five beats of three notes each—a hemiola effect can be obtained by writing two groups of five ♪ notes each. This rhythmic effect Carter incorporated in his *Double Concerto* (Ex. 3-21).

Ex. 3-21. Elliott Carter: *Double Concerto*, p.34

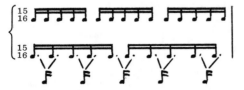

The consistent dotting of quintuplet and septuplet figures in compound time signatures, observable in many of Carter's late works, is not the only unusual aspect of the music. Surely his are among the most complex scores of our time, both rhythmically and notationally. Their complications, plus the composer's almost obsessive compulsion for highly intricate and supposedly unequivocal notation, present the performer with as many interpretive problems as works offering complete freedom of choice among a number of parametral permutations. The *Double Concerto*, the *Piano Concerto*, the *Concerto for Orchestra*, and all three string quartets bring to mind Schoenberg's remark—

applied to his own music—that such music must be realized with "inexorable severity." The players of Carter's works cannot "interpret" the music; they can only follow as best they can his minutely conceived and rapidly fluctuating indicia. The scores, as they stand, vividly illustrate the pitfall into which the over-zealous notator can tumble: their hyperexactitude becomes more inhibiting than the most calculated obscurity. This is especially true of the rhythmic notation; Carter has made his performers' task more rather than less difficult by his insistence on a form of notation both overly fussy and, at times, metrically incorrect.

As an attempt to clear up the confusion and disagreement concerning the writing of all irrational note groups within the limitations of compound time, Ex. 3-22 demonstrates the proper forms for each. The first column presents the precise and noncontroversial versions of each irrational figure; the next column shows an acceptable alternative notation (when possible). Both formats are the durational equivalents of the notations in the right-hand column. The meters illustrated are $\frac{3}{8}$–$\frac{15}{8}$; compound time signatures with smaller or larger denominational values would require adjustment in accordance with the values used for the irrational figures.

To composers whose musical credo is solidly rooted in ametrical or the newer proportional notation, the question of "right" and "wrong" in the writing of irrational groups within established meters can have little relevancy. For those composers still honoring the precepts of traditional rhythmic notation, however, the question does have pertinence; and the solutions to that question are thoroughly viable in contemporary rhythmic practice and its written forms.

In Irregular Meters

Ironically, irrational rhythmical subdivisions of the primary beats within irregular meters are notated more logically and simply than those occurring in compound time. If disagreement exists among composers as to the proper form of these notations, their contention is muted. This is not because the technique is rarely used; on the contrary, in contemporary music that still relies on metrical organization, irregular meters and irrational note groups alike are extensively employed and just as frequently combined. Knowledge of their correct notational formats, therefore, should be of more than academic interest to composers and performers.

Ex. 3-22

a. $\frac{3}{8}$ meter:

	Irrational note group	Alternative notation	Equivalent to
Duplet			
Quadruplet			
Quintuplet			
Septuplet			
Octuplet			
Decuplet			

b. $\frac{6}{8}$ meter:

	Irrational note group	Alternative notation	Equivalent to
Quadruplet			
Quintuplet			

c. $\frac{9}{8}$ meter:

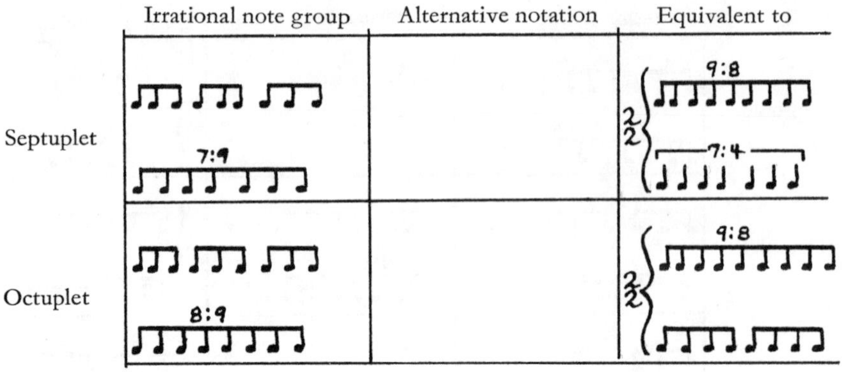

Irrational note group	Alternative notation	Equivalent to
Septuplet		$\frac{2}{2}$ { 9:8 / 7:4
Octuplet		$\frac{2}{2}$ { 9:8

(Septuplet irrational note group labeled 7:9; Octuplet irrational note group labeled 8:9)

d. $\frac{12}{8}$ meter:

Irrational note group	Alternative notation	Equivalent to
Triplet	3	$\frac{4}{4}$ { 3:2
Quintuplet	5	$\frac{4}{4}$ { 5:4
Septuplet	7	$\frac{4}{4}$ { 7:4
Octuplet	8	$\frac{4}{4}$
Nonuplet	9:12	$\frac{4}{4}$ { 9:8
Decuplet	10:12	$\frac{4}{4}$ { 5 5

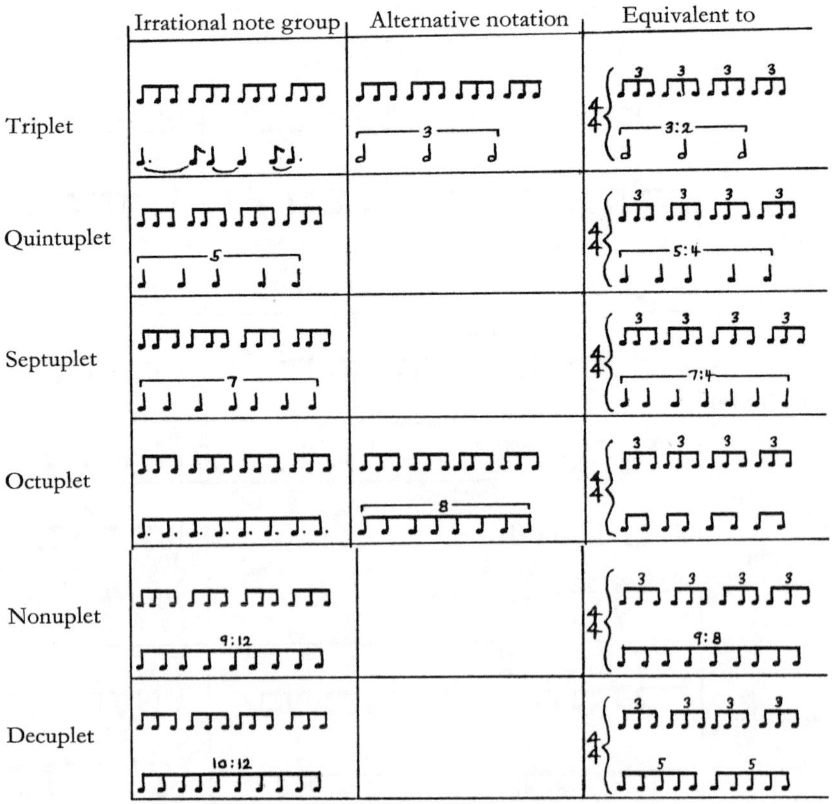

e. $\frac{15}{8}$ meter:

	Irrational note group	Alternative notation	Equivalent to
Duplet		2	$\frac{5}{4}$
Triplet		3	$\frac{5}{4}$
Quadruplet	4		$\frac{4}{4}$ 15:8
Sextuplet	6		$\frac{6}{4}$ 15:12
Septuplet	7		$\frac{7}{4}$ 15:14
Octuplet	8		$\frac{8}{4}$ 15
Nonuplet	9		$\frac{9}{8}$ 15:9
Decuplet	10		$\frac{5}{4}$ 15:10

The principle involved in superimposing unequal rhythmic groups that span whole measures in irregular meters can be briefly stated: the relationships of the opposing time units are mentally reversed in order to determine the proper note values for the irrational group. If, for instance, a triplet is to fill a measure in $\frac{5}{4}$, one thinks of the triplet as the norm (or as a $\frac{3}{4}$ measure), and the irregular meter as the irrational group (a quintuplet in $\frac{3}{4}$). As the latter would be written as five ♩ notes against the normal three ♩'s, a measure triplet in $\frac{5}{4}$ would take the same note values as the basic meter, or three 𝅗𝅥 notes.

Because a quadruplet is the first division of a duplet and an octuplet the first division of quadruplet, it follows that each must be notated with correspondingly shorter values to conform to P2. The same pertains to triplets and sextuplets; the latter must utilize the next shortest note value. In effect, then, P2 supersedes P1 when notating irrational figures larger than the quadruplet in quintuple meters (Ex. 3-25a), the quintuplet in septuple meters (b), and the triplet in meters based on ten (c), eleven (d), and thirteen (e).

In mentally reversing the relationships of an irregular meter and the irrational group contained therein, it is often necessary to consider the latter as also being irrational in a more conventional time signature. For instance: a septuplet in $\frac{5}{8}$ would assume an equivalent relationship in $\frac{3}{8}$ (see Ex. 3-25a). The choice of $\frac{3}{8}$ rather than $\frac{6}{8}$ is because we cannot write a septuplet with larger values than a sextuplet; the values of a sextuplet are, of course, determined by its being the first division of a triplet, hence doubled. And obviously neither an octuplet nor a nonuplet can contain longer values than a septuplet.

With but one exception, P2 was faithfully observed by Samuel Barber in the final, toccata movement of his *Piano Concerto* (Ex. 3-23). The measure triplet at *b* should be in ♪ notes rather than in ♩'s.

Ex. 3-23. Samuel Barber: *Piano Concerto*

a. p.137   b. p.89

c. p.137   d. p.92

Every notation listed in the left-hand column of Ex. 3-25 has—theoretically, at least—an alternative format. Many of these alternate versions, however, are so visually complex and cumbersome that their practicality is severely circumscribed. Involving single- and often double-dotted note values, frequently combined with ties, they present an inextricable picture puzzle to the interpreter's eye. One example will suffice to illustrate both the problem and the unarguable necessity for avoiding such visual entanglements: an octuplet spanning a full measure in $\frac{5}{8}$ meter, expressed simply and concisely as shown in the left-hand column of Ex. 3-25, would have to be written alternatively as indicated below (Ex. 3-24). There is no need to belabor the point; a single visual image here is worth any number of words of explication and admonition.

Ex. 3-24

Ex. 3-25

a. $\frac{5}{8}$ meter:

	Irrational note group	Alternative notation	Equivalent to
Duplet			
Triplet			
Quadruplet			
Sextuplet			
Septuplet			
Octuplet			
Nonuplet			

b. $\frac{7}{8}$ meter:

	Irrational note group	Alternative notation	Equivalent to
Duplet			$\frac{6}{8}$ (7:6)
Triplet			$\frac{3}{4}$ (7:6)
Quadruplet			$\frac{3}{4}$ (7:6 4:3)
Quintuplet			$\frac{3}{4}$ (7:6 5:3)
Sextuplet			$\frac{6}{8}$ (7:6)
Octuplet			$\frac{3}{4}$ (7:6 8:6)
Nonuplet			$\frac{3}{4}$ (7:6 3 3 3)

c. $\frac{10}{8}$ meter:

	Irrational note group	Alternative notation	Equivalent to
Duplet			$\frac{2}{2}$ (5:4 5:4)
Triplet			$\frac{2}{2}$ (5:4 5:4 3)

	Irrational note group	Alternative notation	Equivalent to
Quadruplet			5:4 5:4
Sextuplet			5:4 5:4
Septuplet			5:4 5:4
Octuplet			5:4 5:4
Nonuplet			5:4 5:4

d. $\frac{11}{8}$ meter:

	Irrational note group	Alternative notation	Equivalent to
Duplet			11:8
Triplet			11:8
Quadruplet			11:8
Quintuplet			11:8
Sextuplet			11:8
Septuplet			11:8
Octuplet			11:8

	Irrational note group	Alternative notation	Equivalent to
Nonuplet			*11:8* / *9:8* (in $\frac{4}{4}$)

e. $\frac{13}{8}$ meter:

	Irrational note group	Alternative notation	Equivalent to
Duplet			*13:12* (in $\frac{6}{4}$)
Triplet			*13:12* (in $\frac{3}{2}$)
Quadruplet			*13:12* (in $\frac{6}{4}$)
Quintuplet			*13:12*, *5:3* (in $\frac{3}{2}$)
Sextuplet			*13:12* (in $\frac{6}{4}$)
Septuplet			*13:12*, *7:6* (in $\frac{6}{4}$)
Octuplet			*13:12*, *4:3*, *4:3* (in $\frac{6}{4}$)
Nonuplet			*13:12*, *3*, *3*, *3* (in $\frac{3}{2}$)

On-Beat Fractions

In traditional rhythmic frameworks the irrational note groups used by composers almost invariably occupy full beats or sequent combinations of complete time units, whatever the basic meter in operation. Triplets, for instance, would take up a full quarter-note beat in such standard meters as $\frac{2}{4}$, $\frac{3}{4}$, $\frac{4}{4}$, and the like, or would occupy two consecutive beats in these meters. Occasionally one will find a composer of the past calling for a measure triplet in so-called common time, or $\frac{4}{4}$. But whatever the category of irrational figure, or the number of beats it is designated to span, it begins and ends on a full beat or metrical unit.

In much of today's music, composers are organizing various irrational figures so that they literally straddle measure beats, beginning on a certain portion of one time unit and carrying over to a stipulated fraction of the sequent beat. In its simplest form this technique divides irrational figures between primary and secondary pulses; between beats two and three, for instance, in $\frac{4}{4}$ (or $\frac{2}{2}$). Examples of this procedure are quoted in Ex. 3-26. A more sophisticated application of the technique divides the unequal rhythmic figure between beat halves, whether primary-secondary or secondary-primary (Ex. 3-27.) Irrational figures are often divided between other beat fractions, and not necessarily the same fraction of each beat involved (Ex. 3-28). In compound time, with its division of the beat into three units, irrational figures are frequently divided between thirds of each requisite beat (Ex. 3-29).

Ex. 3-26. Simple time. Irrational group divided between secondary and primary measure beats.

a. Milton Babbitt: *All Set*, p.20

b. Easley Blackwood: *Un Voyage à Cythère*, p.8

c. John Cage: *First Construction (in Metal)*, p.16

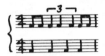

d. Charles Ives: *Robert Browning Overture*, p.13

Ex. 3-27. Simple time. Irrational group divided between beat halves.

a. Milton Babbitt: *All Set*, p.8

b. Milton Babbitt: *Woodwind Quartet*, p.11

c. Jean Barraqué: *Séquence*, p.29

d. Elliott Carter: *Concerto for Orchestra*, p.185

e. Roman Haubenstock-Ramati: *Les symphonies de timbres*, p.18

f. Ibid., p.22

g. Charles Ives: *Symphony no. 4*, p.85

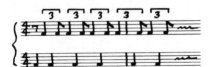

h. Gardner Read: *Sketches of the City*, p.14

i. Dane Rudhyar: *Five Stanzas*, p.9

j. Stefan Wolpe: *Form IV: Broken Sequences*, p.1

k. Stefan Wolpe: *Piece in Two Parts for Six Players*, p.31

Ex. 3-28.   Simple time. Irrational group divided between other beat fractions.

a. Milton Babbitt: *Composition for 12 Instruments*, p.21

b. David Del Tredici: *Syzygy*, p.134

c. Emmanuel Ghent: *Quintet for Brass Instruments*, p.1

d. Ibid., p.4

e. Charles Ives: *In Re Con Moto Et Al*, p.6

and

f. Ibid., p.7

g. Stefan Wolpe: *Piece in Two Parts for Six Players*, p.31

h. Ibid., p.53

i. Ibid., p.63

Ex. 3-29. Compound time. Irrational group divided between beat thirds.

a. Pierre Boulez: *Le marteau sans maître*, p.60

b. Charles Ives: *Symphony no. 4*, p.79

c. Stefan Wolpe: *Quartet for Oboe, Cello, Percussion and Piano*, p.58

Over Barlines

Irrational note groups carried over barlines are not as rare in contemporary music as one might imagine. Some composers, particularly those with experimental predilections, indulge in the technique quite extensively; others view the device more cautiously. Not a few of the scores examined demonstrated but a single instance of an irregular figure straddling a barline in the entire work (Stockhausen's "*Kontra-Punkte*," for example). Certain other scores utilized the technique in a rather sporadic fashion, while a surprising number of compositions—Ives's *Symphony no. 4* being the example *par excellence*—relied on the device heavily. In addition to the fourth symphony and several other scores of Ives, irrational rhythmic groups crossing barlines formed an integral part of the conceptual rhythmic technique of works by Boulez, Babbitt, Cage, Davidovsky, Halffter, and Heider, among others.

Exs. 3-30 through 3-32 organize the trans-barline irrational figures according to their numerical category: duplets, triplets, quadruplets, and so on, up to as many as fifteen units spread between two measures. Ex. 3-30 cites the rhythmic groups that do not entail a change of meter over the barline; Ex. 3-31 presents irrational figures that terminate in a measure with a new time signature; and Ex. 3-32 catalogues irregular note groups spread over two or more full measures, with or without meter changes. Any notes or rests enclosed by parentheses are editorial interpolations that fill out the durational balances of the measures quoted.

Ex. 3-30. Without meter change.

a. **Duplets**

1. Charles Ives: *Symphony no. 4*, p.72

b. **Triplets**

1. Milton Babbitt: *All Set*, p.21

2. Jean Barraqué: *Séquence*
   a. p.1   b. p.29

3. Luciano Berio: *Variazioni per Orchestra da Camera*, p.21

4. Boris Blacher: *Virtuose Musik*, p.17

5. Roman Haubenstock-Ramati: *Ricercare*, p.7

6. Werner Heider: *Plan*, p.23

7. Lejaren Hiller: *String Quartet no. 5*, p.21

8. Charles Ives: *From the Steeples and the Mountains*, p.1

9. Charles Ives: *Robert Browning Overture*, p.85

10. Charles Ives: *String Quartet no. 2*
    a. p.12   b. p.25

11. Charles Ives: *Symphony no. 4*
    a. p.24

    b. p.31

    c. p.31

    d. p.51

    e. p.118

    f. p.175

12. Charles Ives: *Three Places in New England*, p.33
    a.

    b.

13. Shinichi Matsushita: *Correlazioni*, p.5

14. Amadeo Roldan: *Rítmica no. 6*, p.6

15. Dane Rudhyar: *Five Stanzas*, p.20

16. Michael Tippett: *Ritual Dances,* from *The Midsummer Marriage,* p.98

c. **Quadruplets**

1. John Cage: *First Construction (in Metal),* p.2

2. Mario Davidovsky: *Inflexions,* p.35

3. Cristobal Halffter: *Codex I,* p.5

4. Charles Ives: *Symphony no. 4*
   a. p.118

   b. p.147

5. Charles Ives: *Three Places in New England,* p.53

d. **Quintuplets**

1. Alain Bancquart: *Palimpsestes*, p.28

2. Pierre Boulez: *Tombeau*, pp.31–32

3. John Cage: *First Construction (in Metal)*, p.2

4. Mario Davidovsky: *Inflexions*
   a. p.12   b. p.35

   c. p.37

5. Lejaren Hiller: *String Quartet no. 5*, p.20

6. Karel Husa: *Apotheosis of this Earth*
   a. p.12   b. p.15

7. Rudolf Maros: *Eufónia*, p.17

8. Donald Martino: *Concerto for Wind Quintet*, p.13

9. Shinichi Matsushita: *Correlazioni*, p.11

10. Amadeo Roldan: *Rítmica no. 6*, p.7.

11. Karlheinz Stockhausen: "*Kontra-Punkte*," p.58

12. Charles Wuorinen: *Composition for Oboe and Piano*, p.9

e. Septuplets

1. Pierre Boulez: *Tombeau*, p.26

2. Azio Corghi: *In fiěri*, p.29

3. Cristobal Halffter: *Codex I*, p.3

4. Werner Heider: *Plan*
   a. p.8

   b. p.33

5. Rudolf Maros: *Eufónia*, p.17

6. Lawrence Moss: *Remembrances*, p.36

7. Gunther Schuller: *Journey into Jazz*, p.23

f. **Octuplets**
1. Mario Davidovsky: *Inflexions*, p.36

2. Donald Martino: *Piano Concerto*, p.38

g. **Nonuplets**
1. Roque Cordero: *Música veinte*, p.13

2. Mario Davidovsky: *Inflexions*, p.13

3. Werner Heider: *—einander*, p.24

b. **Other values**

1. Pierre Boulez: *Tombeau*, p.59

2. Mario Davidovsky: *Inflexions*, p.13

3. Charles Ives: *Three Places in New England*, p.65

Ex. 3-31. With meter change.

a. **Duplets**

1. Charles Ives: *Symphony no. 4*, p.71

b. **Triplets**

1. Mario Davidovsky: *Inflexions*

    a. p.6

    b. p.9

2. Cristobal Halffter: *In Exspectatione Resurrectionis Domini*, p.3

3. Charles Ives: *Symphony no. 4*, p.37

c. Quintuplets

1. Jean Barraqué: *Séquence*, p.69

2. Iain Hamilton: *Amphion*, p.13

3. Werner Heider: *Plan*, p.12

4. Charles Wuorinen: *Composition for Oboe and Piano*, p.15

d. Septuplets

1. Mario Davidovsky: *Inflexions*, p.12

  a.

  b.

2. Cristobal Halffter: *In Exspectatione Resurrectionis Domini*, p.3

3. Werner Heider: *Plan*, p.12

4. Igor Stravinsky: *Variations: Aldous Huxley in Memoriam*, p.4

Ex. 3-32. Spanning two or more full measures.

a. **Triplets**
1. Jean Barraqué: *Séquence*, p.50

2. Cristobal Halffter: *Brecht-Lieder*, p.2

3. Yoshiro Irino: *Music for 2 Pianos*, p.8

4. William Walton: *Symphony (no. 1)*, p.58

b. **Quadruplets**
1. Cristobal Halffter: *Brecht-Lieder*, p.2

c. **Quintuplets**
1. Boris Blacher: *Collage für Orchester*, p.13

2. Cristobal Halffter: *Brecht-Lieder*, p.2

c. $\frac{1}{8}$

3. Gardner Read: *Symphony no. 2*, p.15

$\frac{3}{8}$

d. **Septuplets**
1. Jean Barraqué: *Séquence*, p.1

$\frac{3}{16}$

2. Cristobal Halffter: *Brecht-Lieder*, p.4

$\frac{1}{8}$

3. Cristobal Halffter: *Codex I*, p.2

$\frac{3}{8}$

e. **Nonuplets**
1. Henry Cowell: *Rhythmicana*, p.3

$\frac{1}{1}$

2. Cristobal Halffter: *Brecht-Lieder*, p.4

$\frac{1}{8}$

f. **Other values**
1. Pierre Boulez: *Tombeau*, p.51

$\frac{2}{4}$

The correct mathematical disposition of an irrational note group spanning a barline and evenly divided between the two measures is to apportion the central note of the group in two halves, tied together, one segment before and one after the barline.[4] Such a proper format is demonstrated, for instance, in Ex. 3-30*b* 3, 4, and 5. Because of ignorance or carelessness, other composers have not always observed this procedure. It cannot be denied, however, that the correct notational form of this technique makes any deviation of rhythmic structure more readily apparent and hence easier to reproduce accurately.

A case in point is the excerpt from an orchestral work by Jurg Baur (Ex. 3-33). As the several different irrational figures spanning barlines do not all begin and end on the same portion of the two measures involved, it would have been clearer had the composer both split his odd-numbered grouplets according to the principle stated above and shown the exact beat fragment for each beginning and ending note.

Dual Irrational Subdivisions

Within the context of single meters, the ultimate in the concept and usage of unequal rhythmic groups is the technique of dual irrational figures. Frequently complicated to notate and usually irksome to decipher, rhythmic figures comprising two levels of irrational values require two simultaneous processes of interpretation. The performer must first relate the primary, overall numeral to the measure beat or beats that it displaces; he or she must then relate the secondary figures—the smaller irregular groupings—to the primary group. In a sense, the larger, comprehensive numeral serves as a new metrical unit; indeed, an actual change of meter can provide a practical solution for most dual irrational situations. For example: a measure triplet in $\frac{2}{4}$ meter that is further subdivided (as in the Messiaen quote, Ex. 3-34*a*), can be notated in $\frac{3}{4}$ to take care of the primary numeral, the $\dot{\quarternote}$ note equalling the $\quarternote$ note of the $\frac{2}{4}$. The resulting polymeter is thus arrived at from the standpoint of simple notational expediency.

In Exs. 3-34 through 3-38 the dual irrational groupings are organized according to the primary value superimposed on the secondary, interior subdivisions. Because of the extreme visual complexity of the example drawn from Stockhausen's piano piece (3-36*c*), a staff has been appended below to show where the primary irrational units of the measure would come in relation to the smaller divisions.

4. Curiously, Donald Harris in his *Ludus* (I) uses this format quite consistently for all irrational figures *within* a single measure. There is no apparent logic for this practice; indeed, it makes the reading more, rather than less, difficult.

Ex. 3-33. Jurg Baur: *Abbreviaturen*, p.12. © 1970 by Breitkopf & Härtel. Used by permission.

Ex. 3-34. Triplets superimposed on various irrational groups.

a. Béla Bartók: *Bluebeard's Castle*, p.33

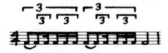

b. Ibid., p.118

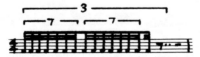

c. Harrison Birtwistle: *Nomos*, p.2

d. Pierre Boulez: *Tombeau*, p.52

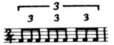

e. Elliott Carter: *Concerto for Orchestra*, p.15

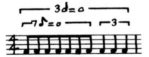

f. David Del Tredici: *Syzygy*, p.26

g. Brian Ferneyhough: *Coloratura*, p.5

h. Brian Ferneyhough: *Missa Brevis*, p.31

i. Brian Ferneyhough: *3 Pieces for Piano*, pp.9, 12

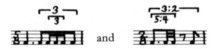

j. Bengt Hambraeus: *Introduzione—Sequenze—Coda*, p.2

k. Ibid., p.5

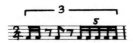

l. Ibid., p.30

m. Donald Harris: *Ludus (I)*, p.8

n. Charles Ives: *Robert Browning Overture*, pp.59, 70

o. Charles Ives: *Symphony no. 4*, pp.34, 85

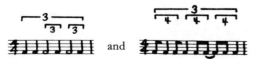

p. Ibid., p.88

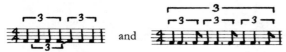

q. Ibid., p.90

r. Ibid., pp.160, 164

s. Ibid., p.154

t. Gyorgy Ligeti: *Atmospheres*, p.11

u. Olivier Messiaen: *Les langues de feu*, from *Messe de la Pentecôte*,
p.2

v. Josep Mestres-Quadreny: *Ibemia*, pp.5, 8

w. Arnold Schoenberg: *Phantasy for Violin and Piano*, p.15

x. Karlheinz Stockhausen: *Klavierstück I*, pp.3, 4

y. William Walton: *Violin Concerto*, pp.106, 107

z. Henry Weinberg: *Cantus Commemorabilis I*, p.25

Ex. 3-35. Quadruplets superimposed on various irrational groups.

a. Bengt Hambraeus: *Introduzione—Sequenze—Coda*, p.19

b. Charles Ives: *Symphony no. 4*, p.4

c. Ibid., p.20

d. Ibid., p.125

e. Gyorgy Ligeti: *Apparitions*, p.20

Ex. 3-36. Quintuplets superimposed on various irrational groups.

a. Bengt Hambraeus: *Introduzione—Sequenze—Coda*, p.3

b. Dane Rudhyar: *Five Stanzas*, p.24

c. Karlheinz Stockhausen: *Klavierstück I*, p.1

d. Karlheinz Stockhausen: *Klavierstück IV*, p.11

Ex. 3-37. Septuplets superimposed on various irrational groups.

a. Elliott Carter: *String Quartet no. 3*, p.13

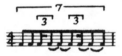

b. Brian Ferneyhough: *3 Pieces for Piano*, p.1

c. Karlheinz Stockhausen: *Klavierstück IV*, p.10

Ex. 3-38. Nonuplets superimposed on various irrational groups.

a. Arnold Schoenberg: *IIIrd String Quartet*, p.23

Typically hyperscrupulous, Schoenberg overnotated his $\frac{2}{2}$-measure nonuplet in 3-38*a*: either the parenthetical $\frac{9}{4}$ meter signature or the superscript numeral 9 would have been sufficient for the problem at hand. Furthermore, his metronomic symbology is in error: a 𝅝. note can represent only six of the nine 𝅗𝅥 notes making up a $\frac{9}{4}$ signature. Therefore the proper relationship should be expressed as: 𝅝. 𝅗𝅥. (total value of the superimposed $\frac{9}{4}$ meter) equals 𝅝 (total value of the basic $\frac{2}{2}$ meter).

A puzzling instance of a misuse of a dual irrational note group occurs in Charles Ives's first string quartet (Ex. 3-39). As the $\frac{4}{4}$ measure is exactly filled by the two 𝅗𝅥 notes and the sequent 𝅘𝅥-note triplet, the superimposed quintuplet numeral is gratuitous. Was this a momentary aberration on the composer's part—or a copyist's slip? One does not know, especially as several measures further on in the score there is a 𝅘𝅥-note quintuplet filling an entire $\frac{4}{4}$ measure, but minus any secondary numeral. This notation, of course, is entirely correct.

Ex. 3-39. Charles Ives: *String Quartet no. 1*, p.16

On the other hand an apparently unnecessary dual irrational marking that appears on page 16 of Elgar's second symphony is, in point of fact, essential. In $\frac{12}{8}$ meter, the final measure beat comprises—quite normally —six ♪ notes, but here phrased in two groups of three notes each. Elgar designates the entire group as a duplet, under which each smaller unit of three notes is marked as a triplet. Thus the momentary hemiola accenting within the established compound time justifies the dual figures used by the composer.

Double irrational note groups have also been carried over barlines in the same manner (but not to the same degree) as single unequal rhythmic figures (Ex. 3-40). Obviously, the barline per se has little, if any, metrical relevance when this is done. The performer's reading problem and interpretive decision are compounded when there is a meter change after the barline, as in the Stravinsky citation (*e*). This is, incidentally, the only instance known to this analyst of Stravinsky's using such an extreme application of rhythmic irrationality.

Ex. 3-40

a. Milton Babbitt: *Partitions*, p.2

b. Charles Ives: *String Quartet no. 2*, p.25

c. Charles Ives: *Symphony no. 4*, p.4

d. Ibid., p.27

e. Igor Stravinsky: *Variations: Aldous Huxley in Memoriam*, p.6

Triple irrational subdivisions are exceedingly rare—and for good reason. Intellectually conceived and requiring a high degree of notational complexity, they defy precise reproduction by the human performer. Furthermore, no human ear, no matter how phenomenally sensitive, can accurately perceive the rhythmic relationships intended. Even on paper one is hard put to untangle the web of irrational values of individual note duration, especially when the nominally operative meter and its constituents are aurally camouflaged beyond all recognition—as in the two excerpts cited in Ex. 3-41.

If one perseveres in dissecting Stockhausen's notation under *b* it will be found that the composer incorrectly notated the primary triplet spanning the entire ¾ measure. This should comprise ♩-note rather than ♪-note units; the smaller segments under each ♩-note of the triplet should be ♪'s and not ♫'s, because they represent second-division values rather than fourth-division.

Ex. 3-41

a. Henryk Gorecki: *Monologhi*, p.19

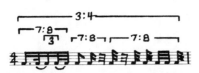

b. Karlheinz Stockhausen: *Klavierstück I*, p.4

Augenmusik, of course, is a rather common manifestation of avant-gardist notational concepts and practices in the music of the late twentieth century. Much metrically based music today, no less than "action" notation, implicit graphics, and similar aleatoric devices, falls within the milieu of "eye music"—valid on its own terms but often presenting insurmountable obstacles to the performer and conductor. Rhythms as intellectually formulated as those shown in many of the examples throughout the book (Ex. 3-41, for instance) are eminently typical of much modern musical thought; they must be met on their own terms if one wishes to decode the rhythmic doctrines of that music. Whether the rewards for so doing are commensurate with the mental effort required is something the individual performer or score reader must determine. And whether or not the performing musician of today can bring computerlike responses to such highly intricate rhythmic notations is decidedly moot. The dilemma is thus two-edged: we cannot dictate what the composer must or must not write; neither can we expect the performer to solve with ease unrealistic notational problems. One suspects that the dilemma will not be quickly resolved.

4

Modern Metrical Concepts
and Their Notations

Unusual Meters

Unusual—or more properly, nonstandard—time signatures are neither new to serious musical expression nor are they restricted to the compositions of this century. Unconventional meters, however, have become so firmly enmeshed in contemporary rhythmic practices that they appear to be unique to the abstruse rhythmic thought in the music of our time. By simple definition, "unusual" would seem to imply a nontraditional and rare usage. But what is unusual or rare for one composer may be the norm for another, so that the term must be further qualified. For the sake of discussion and illustration here, unusual time signatures embrace all meter indications that patently lie outside of the circumscribed group generic to the music of the seventeenth to late nineteenth and early twentieth centuries. Excluded from our listings, however, are certain meter signatures that, unusual though they may be, are now far too commonly employed by contemporary composers to warrant citation ($\frac{1}{16}$, $\frac{2}{8}$, $\frac{9}{4}$, for example). Furthermore, certain imperfect meters based on quintuple and septuple numerator values are now too prevalent to qualify for inclusion—$\frac{5}{2}$, $\frac{7}{16}$, $\frac{10}{4}$, for instance.

In the early years of the present century time signatures such as $\frac{5}{16}$, $\frac{7}{8}$, or $\frac{7}{4}$, among others, were generally regarded as extreme by many composers. Long before the midpoint of the century, however, these and other meters based on the numbers 5, 7, 11, 13, and their multiples were quite frequently utilized by composers, even those whose rhythmic and metrical philosophies were relatively conservative. By the fifties and sixties such metrical frameworks were almost the norm rather than the exception.

A comparison of the ratio between the frequently used time signatures and those more rarely utilized in contemporary music, the latter cited in Appendix A, is both revealing and instructive. Some meters that one would logically assume to be used quite commonly are found but occasionally in current scores; others, which by virtue of their notably small or large numerators, coupled with denominators of extremely short or uncommonly lengthened note values, might be expected to appear infrequently, are found in a surprising number of present-day compositions. Many composers who conspicuously shun the more complex manifestations of metrical subdivision, such as fractional meter, have no hesitation in utilizing time signatures with greatly enlarged numerators, or denominators of the shortest possible note values.

All time signatures based on |○|-note and ○-note denominators, regardless of numerator values, are relatively rare in today's compositions. On the other hand, ♩-note denominators are common coinage in modern time-signature usage. Oddly enough, however, whereas the signatures of $\frac{2}{2}$ to $\frac{6}{2}$ inclusive are overwhelmingly prevalent in twentieth-century scores, $\frac{1}{2}$ is not. Most composers evidently prefer to express this metrical value as $\frac{2}{4}$, even when the established tempo is such that $\frac{1}{2}$ would be a more accurate indicator than $\frac{2}{4}$. Not surprisingly, $\frac{8}{2}$ and $\frac{9}{2}$ are found more rarely than $\frac{5}{2}$ and $\frac{7}{2}$, owing no doubt to the contemporary composer's predilection for quintuple and septuple rhythmic groupings. Indeed, there seem to be more utilizations of $\frac{5}{2}$ as a metrical framework in modern music than of $\frac{6}{2}$, the latter signature being not too far removed from traditional practice.

The time signatures based on ♩-note denominators, their numerators ranging from 1 through 10, are far too common to warrant consideration here. Even the numerators of 11 and 12 over ♩-note denominators are not too rare, but above these numbers the instances of use drop off sharply. Only a bare handful of scores utilizing occasional measures of $\frac{13}{4}$ and higher could be readily located. A consensus of opinion among contemporary composers, though officially uncanonized, would seem to state: the larger the numerator value the smaller the denominator.

The smaller time units, from ♪ notes to ♬ notes, are notably conspicuous as denominator values in twentieth-century music. All signatures based on the ♪ note are now almost more common than those whose denominators represent larger time values. Whereas composers have understandably hesitated to use consistently such top-heavy meter signatures as $\frac{12}{2}$ or $\frac{15}{4}$, let us say, they have not been as reluctant to call for signatures such as $\frac{18}{8}$ or $\frac{21}{8}$—or even $\frac{33}{8}$ (Ives). The prize for inflated numerators, however, must surely be bestowed on

Stockhausen: his *Klavierstück IX* calls for $\frac{34}{8}$, $\frac{42}{8}$, $\frac{87}{8}$, and $\frac{142}{8}$! The composer's unassailable justification is quite simple: these signatures are merely shorthand formats for indicating greatly extended and inflexible repetitions of certain chordal structures, without any interior or secondary accentuations. In addition the device is a welcome and quite necessary means of conserving horizontal space on the score page. Stockhausen has merely written out the first few pulsations of his different vertical structures, indicating by means of an arrow symbol attached to a primary beam that the chord repetitions continue for the time duration specified.

One curious fact, at least, has emerged from our survey of rhythmic practice in the twentieth century: whereas contemporary musical literature is replete with requisitions of $\frac{1}{8}$ and $\frac{2}{8}$ as temporal indicators, their exact equivalents, $\frac{2}{16}$ and $\frac{4}{16}$, are far more rarely used. Why this is so is unclear, especially knowing the demonstrated fondness of modern composers for short-valued denominators. On the other hand, $\frac{3}{8}$ and its equivalent $\frac{6}{16}$ are extremely common, but $\frac{8}{16}$ is not called for as often as its counterpart, $\frac{4}{8}$. In addition, the signatures of $\frac{5}{16}$, $\frac{7}{16}$, and even $\frac{11}{16}$ appear more frequently in modern scores than do the seemingly more conventional meters of $\frac{9}{16}$, $\frac{12}{16}$, and $\frac{15}{16}$. There are less frequent, more sporadic, instances of meter signatures bearing numerator factors higher than 12 over ♪-note denominators. It is not at all surprising that the signature with the largest numerator, $\frac{33}{16}$, was found in a work of Charles Ives, a composer whose scores constitute a veritable thesaurus of advanced rhythmic concept and practice.[1]

Examples of ♪-note denominators are more extensive than one might anticipate, their numerators ranging all the way from 1 to 30 (again, Stockhausen). There are occasional gaps in the numerator factor: in the contemporary publications perused no instances were discovered of $\frac{16}{32}$, $\frac{22}{32}$, $\frac{23}{32}$, or $\frac{26-29}{32}$. Time signatures based on the ♪ note are the type least utilized. A glance at the listings in Appendix A will reveal only eight examples of such signatures, an extremely low percentage among the theoretical possibilities and in comparison with the more extensive appearance of ♪-note and ♪-note denominator values. The avoidance of ♪-note meters may possibly be a matter of notational expediency; the constant presence of note groups containing four or more ligatures not only unduly clutters a score page but also is irksome

---

1. Precedence for large numerators over ♪-note denominators can be traced back at least to J. S. Bach, whose Prelude no. 15 in Book I of the *Well-Tempered Clavichord* bears a signature of $\frac{24}{16}$ in one hand over $\frac{4}{4}$ in the other.

to write. Even the most professional composers, not to mention the performers who play their music, can be intimidated by the visual aspect of a thickly forested page of minimal note values.

Appendix A groups the various meters according to their denominator values, from ○ note through ♪ note. Numerator values are scaled from small to large within each category.

Additive Meters

Theorists and composers of the twentieth century have conceptualized several different, though considerably interrelated, categories of musical meters. These various categories are commonly identified as variable, alternating, combined, additive, mixed, fractional, and simultaneous (polymeters).

Variable meters—often called multimeters—consist of unpatterned changes of time signature, which can be either sporadic or fairly consecutive. The German composer Boris Blacher has termed his own peculiar and personal organization of time signature sequence as "variable meter," but his methodology is based on mathematically derived patterns of meter-numerator increment and subtraction. Cyclical alternations such as 2–3–4–3–4–5–4–5–6–5–6–7, and so on, or 2–3–5–8–13–8–5–3–2 (the Fibonacci series), and similar permutations of numerical order are typical of Blacher's conceptual arrangement of variable meter. The majority of present-day composers, however, reserve the "variable meter" appellation for random changes of time signature.

A composer who chooses two time signatures, such as $\frac{2}{4}$ and $\frac{3}{8}$, and repeatedly alternates between them in a series of paired measures is using "alternating meters." There are, of course, variations to this practice; a composer may use the format of alternating meter to mean unsystematized alternations between the two signatures. In other words, two measures of $\frac{2}{4}$ might be followed by three measures of $\frac{3}{8}$, succeeded in turn by one of $\frac{2}{4}$, followed by two of $\frac{3}{8}$, and so on. An example of this procedure appears in Hindemith's wind quintet (see page 1 and following of the score).

Combined meters juxtapose or freely alternate measures containing the same number of units in simple and compound time—$\frac{3}{4}$ and $\frac{6}{8}$, for example. The technique is a notationally convenient way to utilize hemiola on a more than casual or incidental basis (see, for instance, the excerpt from Vaughan Williams's sixth symphony, Ex. 5-51).

Because variable, alternating, and combined meters pose no notational problems, they are not illustrated in these pages. Additive,
mixed, and fractional meters, however, are fully discussed and demonstrated, because they represent the newer concepts regarding metrically
derived rhythmic structures and raise rather special questions as to
their notation and interpretation.

Additive meters [2] are used to notate unorthodox arrangements of
the components within standard time signatures. In conventional
usage the ♪ notes of a $\frac{4}{4}$ meter, for instance, outline an interior pattern
of $2+2+2+2$ or of $4+4$, following the normal stresses of the measure.
This would be true even if the pairs of ♪ notes were further subdivided
into either regular or irregular arrangements, as in Ex. 4-1.

Ex. 4-1

Applying the concept of additive meter to $\frac{4}{4}$ (or $\frac{8}{8}$), the interior unit
patterns might be $3+3+2$, $3+2+3$, $2+3+3$, $5+3$, $3+5$, and so on.
In simple terms, then, any theoretical pattern of the eight ♪'s (or further
subdivisions) of a $\frac{4}{4}$ measure that does not duplicate the normal interior
arrangements would constitute an additive metrical framework.

As our principal concern here is with the notational rather than the
compositional or stylistic problems related to additive meters, Ex. 4-2
serves merely to illustrate the most commonly utilized formats for this
particular metrical device. Of the ten forms shown, that under *c* is the
most succinct; it is not surprising, therefore, that the great majority of
contemporary composers prefer it to the others shown.

Ex. 4-2

---

2. Some theorists, including this author in *Music Notation: A Manual of Modern
Practice*, have termed this technique "compound" meter, but the alternative
designation is used here to ensure that it is not confused with compound time.

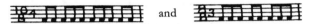

Two early twentieth-century composers in particular designated additive meters in their scores in rather nonconformist manners (Ex. 4-3). The smaller figure in the time signatures of the French composer-conductor Inghelbrecht indicates the number of irregular rhythmic groupings within the measure. Only by examining the interior beamings of the measure do we learn that the groupings are arranged in patterns of unequal duration. Dane Rudhyar's time signature is more obvious—two $\frac{5}{8}$ measures combined as one $\frac{5}{4}$ measure equally divided.

Ex. 4-3

a. Desiré E. Inghelbrecht: *El Greco*, pp.1, 2

b. Dane Rudhyar: *Five Stanzas*, p.9

Additive meter disguised as polymeter characterizes one particular passage in Bruno Bartolozzi's string quartet (Ex. 4-4). Against a consistent $\frac{4}{4}$ pattern in the cello, the composer pits changing measures of $\frac{5}{8}$ and $\frac{3}{8}$ in the other instruments. This is only an alternative way of indicating $5 + 3$ and $3 + 5$ in the basic $\frac{4}{4}$, as demonstrated editorially on the uppermost staff of the citation.

Ex. 4-4. Bruno Bartolozzi: *Quartetto per archi*, p.6

The question naturally arises: has Bartolozzi made the rhythmic solution more or less difficult by his notation? Inasmuch as the polymetric patterns are random but, at the same time, the ♩-note and ♪-note time units are consistently used, it might have been notationally simpler—yet just as clear in intent—to use an additive meter format rather than a polymetric one.

On the other hand, composers sometimes have specified additive meters that are essentially meaningless; that is, the format chosen to express a compound arrangement of rhythmic units actually represents the standard and expected patterns within that particular measure's boundaries. A clear case in point occurs in Harrison Birtwistle's *Entr'actes and Sappho Fragments*, page 12 of the score: the composer here notated a $\frac{3+3+3}{16}$—the normal arrangement of a $\frac{9}{16}$ meter. In this same work (page 35) the composer also notated a $\frac{3+1}{4}$—again, a rather meaningless subterfuge for $\frac{4}{4}$.

Even in the music of Béla Bartók, who was one of the most avid practitioners of additive meter, the total units of time-signature numerators seldom exceed twelve. Anthony Gilbert's *Sonata for Piano* offers a rare instance of a number of topheavy numerator factors in additive meter formats: $\frac{7+7+10}{16}$, $\frac{9+9+9}{16}$, $\frac{11+11+8}{16}$, and $\frac{13+13+7}{16}$ (see Trio I of the third movement).

It seems safe to assert that of the many and varied metrical techniques present in the serious music of our day, that based on an additive principle is one of the most pervasive. Clear in its intent, simply notated, and easily comprehended by the performer, additive meter will no doubt animate much of the mainstream musical expression of the years to come.

Mixed Meters

A mixed meter is the combination within a single measure of dual time signatures having different denominators: $\frac{2}{4}+\frac{3}{16}$, for example. The pair of denominators is usually at the ratio of 1:2, 1:4, or 1:8. In other words, such meters as $\frac{2}{4}+\frac{1}{8}$, $\frac{3}{4}+\frac{3}{16}$, and $\frac{4}{4}+\frac{5}{32}$ represent the norm for mixed-meter practice. Theoretically, numerator ratios may be at any level whatsoever, although they do not, as a practical rule, exceed the factor of 1:5 (as in $\frac{1}{4}+\frac{5}{16}$). Elliott Carter's signature of $\frac{3}{8}+\frac{12}{32}$ in his third string quartet adheres to the common practice, demonstrating a 1:4 ratio in both numerator and denominator.

When the denominator ratio is 1:2, mixed meters can serve as alternative notations for additive meters. For instance, the time signature of $\frac{2}{4}+\frac{3}{8}$ is only another, equally valid, manner of indicating $^{4+3}_{\ 8}$, and $\frac{3}{8}+\frac{2}{16}$ is an alternative notation for $^{6+2}_{16}$. When, however, other ratio factors are in operation, mixed meter cannot convincingly act as a surrogate for additive meter. To illustrate: $\frac{2}{4}+\frac{3}{16}$ is not a viable substitute for $^{8+3}_{16}$, as a primary beat slow enough to distinguish the component ♪ notes would in all likelihood require a signature of $\frac{4}{8}+\frac{3}{16}$—if not $\frac{11}{16}$, depending upon internal accentuations.

The question naturally occurs to the composer and theorist: why not write two separate measures with changing meters rather than only one measure combining two signatures? If the composer desires the metrical pattern of $\frac{2}{4}+\frac{3}{16}$, what disadvantages accrue, if any, in splitting the pattern between two separate and autonomous measures? Why should one measure of mixed meter be superior to two measures bearing individual time signatures?

The principal disadvantage of expressing mixed meter in a variable meter format may seem minor to some musicians but it is crucial to the rhythmic problem involved. A solid barline following the initial measure with but one time signature implies a primary accent in the second measure, which bears a new meter sign. This is not at all what mixed meter signifies: the second of the dual time signatures is always intended as an appendage to the first signature; it is not to be its equal in terms of stress. The distinction may be subtle but it is far from being academic. The $\frac{3}{16}$ of the mixed meter used here as an abstract example is an adjunct to the $\frac{2}{4}$ signature; it is not considered, nor should it be interpreted, as an equally stressed time unit in relation to the initial pattern of component ♪ notes. Rather, the secondary $\frac{3}{16}$ meter sign should be regarded as an added fraction of the basic ♩-note unit, requiring a corresponding secondary accentuation.

To demonstrate each mixed-meter denominator ratio in turn, as utilized by composers of the twentieth century, the tables in the first half of Appendix B illustrate the ratios of 1:2, 1:4, and 1:8, with their respective numerators increasing in values from minimum to maximum. In the second half of Appendix B, the ratios are reversed, with the lesser denominator preceding the greater.

As with all metrical categories, mixed-meter denominators can be designated with noteheads in lieu of numerals, as Stockhausen chose to do in his *Mixtur* (Ex. 4-5a). Mixed-meter signatures may also combine notehead and numerical denominators, particularly when the former represent compound time and the latter simple time, as at 4-5b.

Ex. 4-5

a. Karlheinz Stockhausen: *Mixtur*

b. Charles Wuorinen: *Adapting to the Times*

Mixed meters comprising three contrasting signatures are relatively rare. It is more feasible—at least from a notational standpoint—to divide such triple rhythmic patterns into only two meters, uniting either the first or the last two signatures as a single measure. This procedure is more sensible than attempting to accommodate all three meters within a single pair of barlines.

Exs. 4-6 and 4-7 list the comparatively few instances of the contemporary composer's reliance on tripartite mixed meters. First given are the examples that call for only two different denominator note values; following are those that require three different denominator values.

Ex. 4-6. Two denominator values.

a. Bo Nilsson: *Mädchentotenlieder*

b. Shinichi Matsushita: *Le Croîture Noir*

c. Edgard Varèse: *Déserts*

d. Bo Nilsson: *Stunde eines blocks*

e. Peter Maxwell Davies: *Five Motets*; Leon Kirchner: *Concerto for Violin, Cello, Ten Winds and Percussion*; Shinichi Matsushita: *Canzona da sonare no. 1*

$\frac{3}{8} + \frac{2}{4} + \frac{3}{8}$ ( )

f. Michael Tippett: *Symphony no. 2*

$\frac{3}{8} + \frac{2}{8} + \frac{3}{16}$ ( )

g. Donald Harris: *Ludus II*

$\frac{3}{8} + \frac{5}{16} + \frac{3}{8}$ ( )

Ex. 4-7. Three denominator values.

a. Karlheinz Stockhausen: *Mixtur*

$\frac{2}{\text{P}} + \frac{1}{\circ} + \frac{4}{\text{P}}$ ( )

b. Jean Barraqué: *Séquence*

$\frac{3}{16} + \frac{1}{4} + \frac{1}{8}$ ( )

Parenthetically, but perhaps necessarily, too, performers might be cautioned here not to confuse the formats of mixed and of combined meters, which, on first glance, appear deceptively similar. Mixed meters always have—or should have—a plus sign (+) between the dual time signatures. Combined meters, on the other hand, assume one or the other of the seven formats demonstrated in Ex. 4-8. The meter chosen as exemplar indicates combined or alternating compound and simple time; it does not signify the mixed meter of $\frac{12}{16}$ plus $\frac{2}{4}$. Of the variants shown, that under *c* is clearest and least controversial.

Ex. 4-8

Fractional and Decimal Meters

Fractional meters and their notational counterparts, decimal meters, are indisputably unique by-products of the complex rhythmic premises of twentieth-century music. All rhythm and meter, of course, is based on the science of mathematics; hence fractional meters and rhythms are quite natural extensions of this conceptuality. The numerical fraction per se also explains the notation of meter signs as fractions, a time-signature format favored by many contemporary composers (see Ex. 2-18).

Musicologists, of course, delight in reminding us that fractions played an important role in the rhythmic structures of fifteenth- to seventeenth-century manuscripts. A $\frac{9}{8}$ or a $\frac{3}{2}$, for instance, as found in many of these early compositions, was not a meter signature in the modern sense but a proportional indication of time: the measures following these particular fractions would contain nine time units in the previous space of eight, or three in the time of two. An $\frac{8}{9}$ or a $\frac{2}{3}$ appearing later in the music would then indicate a return to the original number of time units: eight in the span of nine or two in the duration of three. The musical effect would be a quickening and subsequent slowing of tempo, according to a very exact ratio. It would thus appear that the seeds of Elliott Carter's twentieth-century "metric modulation" reside in a tradition widely observed in early mensural notation.

Fractional and mixed meters are closely interrelated, the one being but an alternative version of the other. For example: $\frac{2}{4} + \frac{1}{8}$ is only a different way of writing $\frac{2\frac{1}{2}}{4}$, while $\frac{3\frac{1}{4}}{8}$ is just an alternate notation for $\frac{3}{8} + \frac{1}{32}$. Furthermore, the first fractional signature cited, $\frac{2\frac{1}{2}}{4}$, can also be expressed as a decimal meter: $\frac{2.5}{4}$. The terms mixed, fractional, and decimal, therefore, differentiate only notational techniques and do not signify widely divergent rhythmic or metrical concepts. Nor do the aural results of these notational variants differ perceptibly.

It should be stressed that whereas in mixed meters the smaller of the two or more denominators can appear in either of two positions, e.g., $\frac{2}{4} + \frac{1}{16}$ or $\frac{1}{16} + \frac{2}{4}$, in fractional or decimal meter formats the added portion of the beat or counting unit almost invariably appears at the measure end. Thus, $\frac{4\frac{1}{2}}{4}$ usually means *a* of Ex. 4-9, and not the arrangements under *b* and *c*. These latter subdivisions of the measure, and other comparable internal arrangements, would more properly be expressed in the form of additive meter (see pp.87–90). Even the more extreme fractional additions to the beat are normally found at the end of the measure (*d*) rather than at the beginning or middle (*e* and *f*).

Exceptions, one is forced to add, invariably disprove this contention. We find Charles Wuorinen utilizing the signature of $\frac{4\frac{1}{4}}{4}$ in one of his works but dividing the fraction of the beat into two segments, located as shown in Ex. 4-10. Admittedly, this is an extreme manipulation of a metrical beat fraction. But it illustrates an approach to

Ex. 4-9

rhythmic complexity that is highly characteristic not only of Wuorinen personally but also of twentieth-century composers as a class.

Ex. 4-10. Charles Wuorinen: *The Long and the Short*, p.4

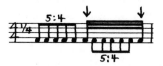

The actual format of indicating fractional meter has, not surprisingly, undergone several variations in contemporary scores. That of Ex. 4-11*a* is the one most frequently encountered, its directness and simplicity evidently finding favor with the majority of composers. The final signature shown is the decimal equivalent of the other meters. Decimal meters, of course, can only be used when the denominator value (of the upper portion of the signature) is capable of being divided into tenths. For example: whereas $\frac{2\frac{3}{4}}{4}$ can also be expressed as $\frac{2.6}{4}$, the meter fraction of $3\frac{3}{4}$ cannot be so translated. When decimals other than .5 are used, the denominator value must be extended by a portion of an irrational rhythmic figure, as illustrated in Ex. 4-12. Because of these inherent restrictions decimal meters are more limited in practical application than their fractional counterparts; consequently they are found but rarely, even in the most rhythmically rigorous of contemporary compositions.

Ex. 4-11

Ex. 4-12. Joseph Byrd: *Andromeda*, p.1

Theoretically speaking, any fraction whatsoever can be applied over a time-signature denominator; pragmatically, few composers have gone beyond divisions by two, by three, or by five (and their multiples), as demonstrated in the tables that constitute Appendix C. These citations, of course, represent the first species of fractional meter, in which the fraction is added to the numerator.

In the second species of fractional meter the numerator itself is a fraction. This means that the entire measure consists of only a designated portion of the fundamental beat (the denominator)—not its totality. A signature of $\frac{2/3}{4}$, for example, would represent two-thirds of a basic ♩-note unit or "counter"; in other words, it would comprise two out of three ♪-note triplet units:

The temporal result is a sudden accelerando, but one that is mathematically calculated as to its rate of tempo increase. The following beat, over the barline, thus falls on the durational point vacated by the missing portion of the triplet.

Ex. 4-13 catalogues the recent compositions that utilize this secondary species of fractional meter. Ex. 4-14 illustrates a more puzzling notation of the technique, in which the fractional meter sign is supplemented by an irrational note group indication. To comment specifically on one of Wuorinen's dual signatures (4-14a): clarification from the composer reveals that the first of the bracketed numerals over the small noteheads (the figure 2) represents the number of irrational units that replace the "normal" number of units to occupy the truncated measure. Wuorinen further explains: "I use the brackets as well as the meter signatures because, although the meter signature shows how big the measure is, it doesn't affect the value of notes inside it." The figure 4 represents the total number of units (four triplet ♪'s, notated below as a ♩ note) that are to replace two and two-thirds normal ♪'s. The remaining dual meter signatures would be interpreted in similar fashion.

Ex. 4-13

a. Pierre Boulez: *Le marteau sans maître*, p.93; Bo Nilsson: *Mädchentotenlieder*, p.10

b. Pierre Boulez: Ibid., p.17

$$\tfrac{4/3}{2} =$$

c. Ibid., p.18; Roman Haubenstock-Ramati: *Ricercari*, p.3; Bo Nilsson: Ibid., p.12

$$\tfrac{2/3}{4} =$$

d. Bo Nilsson: Ibid., p.10

$$\tfrac{3/5}{4} =$$

e. Ibid., p.11

$$\tfrac{4/5}{4} =$$

Ex. 4-14

a. Charles Wuorinen: *Composition for Oboe and Piano*, p.12

$$2 \quad 4{:}2\tfrac{2}{3}$$

b. Ibid., p.13

$$4 \quad 8{:}5\tfrac{1}{2}$$

c. Charles Wuorinen: *Sonata for Piano*, p.11

$$\tfrac{1}{3} =$$

d. Charles Wuorinen: *Bicinium*, p.3

$$2 \quad 2{:}1\tfrac{1}{3}$$

e. Charles Wuorinen: *Sonata for Piano*, p.10

$$\tfrac{5}{3} =$$

Further rhythmic complications may be added to those inherent in fractional time signatures by combining these signatures with other metrical arrangements, such as mixed meter. Thus we find in Exs. 4-15, 16, and 17 certain amalgams of standard and fractional meters, as required by three mid-twentieth-century composers. Several of the citations (4-15c, d, and e, and all of 4-16 and 17) give the effect of a fractional beat within a measure governed by a single time signature, inasmuch as the denominators in each case are the same for all meters involved. In one sense these fractional portions of a meter produce the equivalent of a sudden, brief accelerando on the measure beat affected, but one that is achieved in strict mathematical terms.

Ex. 4-15. Bo Nilsson: *Mädchentotenlieder*

a. p.1:

b. p.8:

c. p.8:

d. p.9:

e. p.11:

Ex. 4-16. Charles Wuorinen: *Sonata for Piano*

a. p.12:

b. p.30:

Ex. 4-17. Donald Martino: *Piano Fantasy*, p.8

a.

b.

c.

The explicit premise of fractional rhythm does not apply solely to metrical arrangements affecting entire measures. The technique can be requisitioned for individual beats or measure units within any conventionally stipulated meter or in music organized *senza misura* (such as John Cage's *Music of Changes*). Fractional rhythm can be applied not only to pitch duration but also to rests or to combinations of note duration and silence. Furthermore, the concept of irrational note grouping can be superimposed on that of fractional rhythm, so that a given fraction of a metrical beat is itself further fragmented by being organized into an unequal note group (Ex. 4-18). The ultimate application of this concept would doubtless be to carry the mixture of fractional beat and irrational rhythm over a barline, with the meter changing in the second measure!

Ex. 4-18. Emmanuel Ghent: *Quintet for Brass Instruments*

Appendix D cites the instances of fractional rhythmic use in various scores by twentieth-century composers. The fractions required are listed from $\frac{1}{3}$ and its multiples to $\frac{3}{8}$.

New Rhythmic Proposals

Rhythmical and metrical experimentation—sometimes sporadic, often sustained—have been characteristic of every period in the history of Western music. It seems safe to assert, however, that the present century has witnessed the most intensive and widespread preoccupation with the rhythmic parameter in musical expression. Because of the contemporary composer's dissatisfaction with traditional notation and its obvious inability to delineate nontraditional rhythmic and metrical formulae, innumerable proposals have been advanced throughout the century, seeking to extend the boundaries both of primary rhythmic concepts and of their concomitant symbological formats. Some of these proposals have exerted considerable force on the shaping and the refinement of late twentieth-century rhythmical components; others have had only a peripheral influence, if any, on the rhythmic and metrical practices of our time.

As Henry Cowell pointed out so eloquently during the earliest decades of the century, our traditional system of orthochronic[3] notation contains no denominator symbol capable of irregular sub-division. Though we can divide simple duple time by two and its multiples and both simple triple and compound time by three and its multiples, we cannot reverse the process without recourse to either irrational figures or the awkward expedient of various tied notes. Neither can we divide either simple or compound time into five, seven, eleven, or thirteen, for instance, without the mandatory use of ancillary numerals and their accompanying brackets and the tying together of unequal note values.

The signal failure of our standard time signatures to cope with irregular time units can be demonstrated by the simple problem of notating a measure of five equal ♪ notes that are to receive one primary, comprehensive beat. One has to notate this elementary numerical construct either as an artificial division within a conventional meter:

or by tying together two different note values in an irregular meter:

In the latter case the signature obviously fails to represent the true metrical feeling, as it denotes not the combined value of five ♪ notes but only the individual number of such units within the measure. The same failure would pertain if the quintuple figure occupied a primary beat in simple time, such as:

If only modern composers had recourse to single denominator symbols

3. From the Greek *ortho* ("correct") and *chronos* ("time"); hence correct, or measurable, time.

that would serve to express irregular patterns of meter and pulse, their notational labors would be made immeasurably easier.

It is ironic that although such symbols have been proposed, today's composers have not as yet made them a part of their technical arsenal. In Henry Cowell's system, first put into practice in his 1917 piano piece *Fabric*, and later expounded in his pioneering *New Musical Resources* (1919), a quintuple value—as one example—would be expressed by means of a square-shaped note, stemmed and flagged according to traditional notational principles (see Ex. 4-19c). Cowell's new symbol is intended to represent not quintuple meter but only one component of a quintuplet. Five beamed square noteheads, therefore, would constitute an ♪-note quintuplet in either simple or compound time—$\frac{2}{4}$, $\frac{3}{4}$, $\frac{3}{8}$, or $\frac{6}{8}$— thus obviating the addition of an irrational numeral and bracket over the note group.

Employed in a metrical context, quintuple values or their multiples would be expressed as 5, 10, 20, or 40 (the denominator) under whatever numerator value the composer chooses. $\frac{6}{5}$, for instance, would represent a full measure consisting of six fifth notes, which could, of course, be further subdivided into tenth, twentieth, or fortieth values.

In explaining his system Cowell pointed out the close relationships that exist between the various series of note values and his proposed notehead formats. For example: third, sixth, twelfth, twenty-fourth and forty-eighth notes belong to one fractional "scale" and hence their notational equivalents are correspondingly related. So too are eleventh, twenty-second and forty-fourth notes comparable in their notational representations, and so on for each one of the new durational series proposed. Each odd number and its successive division by two, therefore, creates a new fractional series and a different but correlative note shape. Stems, flags, and beams are added to the noteheads according to traditional procedures and the smaller values, analogous to ♪'s through ♬'s, have solid rather than open symbols.

In Cowell's *Quartet Romantic* for two flutes, violin, and viola, also completed in 1917, when the composer-experimenter was only twenty, all the durations are formulated according to the ratios derived from the pitch vibrations of the overtone series. Thus one finds such unorthodox—and fascinating—juxtapositions as $6\frac{2}{3}$ over $5\frac{1}{3}$ over 4 over $2\frac{2}{3}$, and $7\frac{1}{2}$ over 6 over $2\frac{1}{4}$ over $4\frac{1}{2}$. The quartet makes liberal use of Cowell's shaped noteheads to express such values as $\frac{2}{3}$, $\frac{3}{5}$, $\frac{4}{13}$, $\frac{2}{15}$, and other such nontraditional note lengths. It is interesting to observe that Cowell conceived his polyrhythmic constructs primarily on the basis of full rather than partial measures.

A somewhat different proposal was put forward in 1961 by the Italian composer and theorist Bruno Bartolozzi;[4] he would have the value of five ♪'s expressed by means of a double stem attached to a half note, one stem flagged, the other not (Ex. 4-20*a*). Read's *Music Notation: A Manual of Modern Practice* (first edition, 1964), suggested that by flagging a single half-note stem, the value of four ♪ notes (♩) plus one ♪ note ( ) could be expressed (Ex. 4-21*a*). Thus the two proposals have a single goal in mind: to represent an irregular metrical unit by a single new symbological device with traditional antecedents.

Inasmuch as fifth notes constitute only one out of the array of irregular time units possible, the remaining fractional values as proposed by Cowell, Bartolozzi, and this writer are demonstrated in Exs. 4-19 to 21 inclusive, for purposes of comparison and personal evaluation.

Ex. 4-19. Henry Cowell's proposed system. © 1922, renewed 1950 by Breitkopf Publications, Inc. Used by permission.

Whole-Note Series
Oval-shaped notes
a. Whole-note: ○ half-note: ♩ quarter-note: ♩ 8th-note: ♪ 16th-note: ♪ 32nd-note: ♪

Third-Note Series
Triangular-shaped notes
b. 2-3rds-note: △ 3rd-note: ♩ 6th-note: ♩ 12th-note: ♪ 24th-note: ♪ 48th-note: ♪

Fifth-Note Series
Square notes
c. 4-5ths-note: □ 2-5ths-note: ♩ 5th-note: ♩ 10th-note: ♪ 20th-note: ♪ 40th-note: ♪

Seventh-Note Series
Diamond-shaped notes
d. 4-7ths-note: ◇ 2-7ths-note: ♩ 7th-note: ♩ 14th-note: ♪ 28th-note: ♪ 56th-note: ♪

Ninth-Note Series
Oblong notes
e. 8-9ths-note: ▭ 4-9ths-note: ♩ 2-9ths-note: ♩ 9th-note: ♪ 18th-note: ♪ 36th-note: ♪

Eleventh-Note Series
Oval notes with stroke
f. 8-11ths-note: ♩ 4-11ths-note: ♩ 2-11ths-note: ♩ 11th-note: ♪ 22nd-note: ♪ 44th-note: ♪

Thirteenth-Note Series
Triangular notes with stroke
g. 8-13ths-note: ♩ 4-13ths-note: ♩ 2-13ths-note: ♩ 13th-note: ♪ 26th-note: ♪ 52nd-note: ♪

Fifteenth-Note Series
Square notes with stroke
h. 8-15ths-note: ♩ 4-15ths-note: ♩ 2-15ths-note: ♩ 15th-note: ♪ 30th-note: ♪ 60th-note: ♪

Intriguing though these several rhythmic proposals might be, there are serious limitations and drawbacks to each. The principal difficulty with Henry Cowell's system, for instance, resides not so much in the

4. See Bibliography.

Ex. 4-20. Bruno Bartolozzi's proposed system

a. $\frac{5}{32}$ [notation] or [notation] $\frac{5}{16}$ [notation] or [notation] $\frac{5}{8}$ [notation] or [notation] $\frac{5}{4}$ [notation] or [notation]

b. $\frac{7}{32}$ [notation] or [notation] $\frac{7}{16}$ [notation] or [notation] $\frac{7}{8}$ [notation] or [notation] $\frac{7}{4}$ [notation]

c. $\frac{9}{32}$ [notation] or [notation] $\frac{9}{16}$ [notation] or [notation] $\frac{9}{8}$ [notation] or [notation] $\frac{9}{4}$ [notation] or [notation]

d. $\frac{10}{32}$ [notation] or [notation] $\frac{10}{16}$ [notation] or [notation] $\frac{10}{8}$ [notation] or [notation] $\frac{10}{4}$ [notation] or [notation]

e. $\frac{11}{32}$ [notation] or [notation] $\frac{11}{16}$ [notation] or [notation] $\frac{11}{8}$ [notation] or [notation] $\frac{11}{4}$ [notation] or [notation]

f. $\frac{13}{32}$ [notation] or [notation] $\frac{13}{16}$ [notation] or [notation] $\frac{13}{8}$ [notation] or [notation] $\frac{13}{4}$ [notation] or [notation]

g. $\frac{14}{32}$ [notation] or [notation] $\frac{14}{16}$ [notation] or [notation] $\frac{14}{8}$ [notation] or [notation] $\frac{14}{4}$ [notation] or [notation]

h. $\frac{15}{32}$ [notation] or [notation] $\frac{15}{16}$ [notation] or [notation] $\frac{15}{8}$ [notation] or [notation] $\frac{15}{4}$ [notation] or [notation]

geometric distinctions of the various noteheads as in the relative sizes of the symbols that delineate the fifth-note and ninth-note series. Read from a distance, as they would be in any orchestral set-up, square and oblong noteheads—not to mention the minute differences in size that characterize first- and second-degree values within each category—are easily confused.

Bartolozzi's series raises similar doubts. His notehead formats are less logical, perhaps, in that he dispenses with distinctions between their various shapes, an element fundamental to Cowell's premise. It would not be difficult to mistake an eleventh–eighth note as a fourteenth–eighth, for instance, or a thirteenth–fourth note as a fifteenth–fourth, their respective symbological distinctions being so microscopic. Of all Bartolozzi's catalogue, only his proposal for septuple time units merits

Ex. 4-21. Gardner Read's proposed system

a. ♩ ♩ or ♩ ♩. or ♩ ♪ │ ♪

b. ♩ ♪ ♩ ♪ │ ♩ ♩

c. ♩ ♩. or ♩. ♩ or ♩. ♪ │ ♪.

d. ♩ ♪ ♩ ♪ │ ♩. ♩.

e. ♩ ♪ │ ♪

f. ♩ ♪ ♩ ♪ │ ♩ ♩

g. ♩. ♪ │ ♪.

h. ♩. ♪ ♩ ♪ │ ♩. ♩.

wholehearted adoption. As denominator values, the doubly dotted notes accurately express septuple measure values; as the combined segments of a septuplet they do the same, obviating the use of tied notes and irrational numerals, and their brackets.

In all honesty I cannot maintain that my own proposals are superior to Cowell's and Bartolozzi's. Their one virtue, perhaps, is that they derive from traditional notation and its familiar signs, but without recourse to the duplicative note stems, flagged or not, of the other systems. The most serious drawback is that only irregular metrical or rhythmical patterns based on the ♪ note (or smaller values by the addition of more flags or beams) can function within my proposed system. Neither ♩-, ♩-, nor o-note values can be accommodated within the visual expression selected, as the basic premise is to attach flags or beams to the ♩ note, resulting in combinations that do not, of course, occur in traditional notation. A single flag placed on a half-note stem is intended to represent either the meter signature of $\frac{5}{8}$ or the combined values of five ♪'s within any meter capable of containing them: $\frac{4}{4}$ ♩. ♪, for instance. Attached to the stem of a ♩. note, a single flag would delineate either septuple time in a signature or a septuplet value (six ♪ notes plus one ♪ note) within other meters able to accommodate them. Two flags on a half-note stem then produce nine ♪-note units (8 + 1), while dual flags on a ♩.-note stem represent a total of thirteen ♪'s (12 + 1).

Still other serious proposals have recently been propounded for extending traditional note lengths by even or odd fractions. In his *Quintet for Brass Instruments*, the American composer Emmanuel Ghent used the system of ancillary signs shown in Ex. 4-22; these were designed to increase the basic note duration by $\frac{1}{4}$ (*a*) and then the fractional addition by another $\frac{1}{4}$, or a total increment of $\frac{5}{16}$ (*b*). Both visual devices parallel the traditional system of single dotting to increase a note value by $\frac{1}{2}$ and double dotting to increase the length by $\frac{3}{4}$.

Ex. 4-22. Emmanuel Ghent's proposed system

The traditional practice of adding ancillary symbols after noteheads to prolong their durations can be applied to my own proposals. The formats shown in Ex. 4-23 delineate possible ways in which third values might be added to conventional note lengths. A single small × following a notehead could represent an increment of $\frac{1}{3}$ of the note's original value. Ex. 4-23*a* shows applications of this device, illustrating equivalent notations first in compound time (♩. + ♪, for instance) and then in simple time (♩ plus a triplet ♪). Honoring the principle of double dotting, a dual × after a notehead would add a further third value to the first fractional increment, or a total of $\frac{4}{9}$ (see Ex. 4-23*b*).

By altering the format of the ancillary sign to a small ○, a fraction of $\frac{1}{5}$ could be added to the original note duration—operable only in simple time, however. A double symbol (○○) would therefore represent the addition of $\frac{6}{25}$ to the notehead it followed.

It should be noted that these specific fractional increments are arbitrary; they merely represent two of the most common irregular time units favored by contemporary composers. The symbols proposed by Emmanuel Ghent and this writer could, quite naturally, represent any other durational fractions desired—as long, that is, as the composer maintained consistency in both values and symbols.

Though the basic premise of these proposals, including Ghent's, is sound, the symbols chosen are more space-consuming than are the traditional dots, especially when used in pairs. In addition, the ○ symbols can easily be mistaken for inadvertently enlarged dots, particularly when they are partially filled in. Moreover, the range of fractions operative within either system is too constricted to be fully useful to

Ex. 4-23. Gardner Read's proposed system

a. (musical notation) etc.

b. (musical notation) etc.

c. (musical notation) etc.

d. (musical notation) etc.

the composer. To be completely effective, any suggested reform must accommodate all fractional additions to basic note values; partial solutions to the problem are no better than no solutions at all.

Despite certain desirable merits incorporated in each of the various rhythmic proposals discussed it is safe to assume that none of them will exert a significant or lasting influence on the continuing development and expansion of rhythmic conceptuality and its notational forms. Yet, at the same time, one should remember that all progress during the long history of Western musical notation has come about because of the profound concern of composers for both logic and clarity in the written forms of their creative expression. There is always the chance that at least one of the many innovations in the field of rhythmic notation mentioned here may, in time, become a standardized procedure or, at the very least, a seminal influence in the establishment of new systems and techniques. What is absolutely certain, however, is that the experimentation and the advancement of new proposals will continue.

No explication of contemporary rhythmic practice and its concomitant notation can possibly overlook the singular contributions of Olivier Messiaen, a composer who has often and eloquently stated that "rhythm is the prime and perhaps the essential part of music." Although Messiaen's unique system of rhythmic augmentation and diminution has had more of a theoretical than a practical influence on late twentieth-century techniques, it is worthy of close scrutiny. Essentially, what Messiaen has attempted to do—in the words of his most celebrated pupil, Pierre Boulez—is "to set up a dialectic of duration by experimenting with hierarchies of note values (variable contrasts between relatively short and relatively long time-values, which in turn may be either odd or even)." This Messiaen has accomplished by devising systems of added values (*valeurs ajoutées*) and randomly or systematically augmented and diminished rhythms (*rythmes augmentés et diminués*). In addition, he has espoused *rythmes non-rétrogradables*, rhythmic patterns that cannot be retrograded (see definition, p.109). Bypassing all standard metrical patterns and writing in an essentially *sans mesure* format (without time signatures) Messiaen bases his rhythmical permutations on "an intuitive feeling for a given short value and its unrestricted multiplication," as explained by Jacques Chailley. In other words, the units of time in Messiaen's music are constantly of unequal duration, thus negating beat and patterned stress.

The juxtaposition of two apparently irreconcilable concepts in Messiaen's works has puzzled many theoretical analysts. His consistent combination of nonretrogradable and palindromic patterns, which strongly imply symmetry, and of added- and diminished-value rhythms, suggesting irregularity, are rationalized by Messiaen as the "irrationality of true rhythm." To some theorists and composers this may seem to beg the question; for others it satisfactorily justifies the apparent rhythmic dichotomy of Messiaen's expression. A rhythmic music, he has said, "is one that disregards repetition, squareness, and regular division; a music that is, in short, inspired by the movement of nature, a movement of free and uneven durations."

Messiaen's basic conception of "added values" is one of fractions rather than wholes. The addition to or subtraction from the primary note values is accomplished not in accordance with our traditional technique of rhythmic augmentation and diminution but rather according to the fractional segments of any given time unit. To augment a ♩. note by $\frac{1}{3}$, as advocated in Messiaen's system, would yield a ♩ note; traditional augmentation on a 1:1 basis would, of course, result in a ♩. note. Further examples are given in Ex. 4-24. Augmented by $\frac{1}{4}$, the

Ex. 4-24

rhythmic pattern of *a* would become that shown at *b*. The pattern at *c* would be transformed into *d* when augmented by the same ratio.

According to Messiaen's concept of fractional manipulation, rhythmical diminution would operate at similar, and nonstandard, ratios. Thus one could diminish a $\quarternote\!\cdot$ note by $\frac{2}{3}$ ($\quarternote$), or a $\quarternote$ note by $\frac{3}{4}$ ($\eighthnote$), to cite two possibilities. Somewhat less straightforward examples would be the diminishing of a $\quarternote$ note by $\frac{1}{3}$

$$(\overset{\ulcorner 3 \urcorner}{\quarternote(\textit{rest})}),$$

or a $\quarternote\!\cdot$ note by $\frac{1}{4}$

$$(\text{♩.♪}).$$

Symmetrical augmentation of certain rhythmic figures, on the other hand, would yield the results demonstrated in Ex. 4-25. The note values of the patterns at *a* are augmented on a traditional 1:1 basis, so that each value is doubled (*b*). The values under *c*, however, are increased by $\frac{3}{4}$ (*d*). The values within the several rhythmic cells at *e* are all increased symmetrically (*f*), while only selected segments within each of the patterns at *g* are augmented in a cumulative manner (*h*).

Ex. 4-25

a. ♫ ♫♪ *b.* ♩. ♫. ♫ (with ⌐3⌐ bracket)

c. ♫♩ ♫. *d.* ♫♫♩... ♫. ♩♫

e. ♪♫ ♫♫♩ *f.* ♫♫. ♫♫♩.

g. ♫♫ ♫♫.♩. *h.* ♫♫ ♫♫.♩. ♫.♩ ♫♩.

An asymmetrical augmentation, as advocated in Messiaen's system, mixes fractional with 1:1 ratios, with results such as the patterns shown in Ex. 4-26. The rhythmic unit at *a*, therefore, could assume the forms given at *b* and *c*, and the pattern at *d* might be augmented as at *e* or *f*.

Ex. 4-26

a. ♫♫. *b.* ♪. ♩ ♩ *c.* ♫. ♩♪

d. ♫♫♫♫ *e.* ♫♫♫♫.♩ *f.* ♫♫♫♪♩♪.

A symmetrical diminution of an arbitrarily chosen figure (Ex. 4-27*a*) would produce the rhythm given at *b*, according to traditional concepts. Fractionally diminished by $\frac{1}{4}$, pattern *c* would appear as *d*. The more extended patterns of *f* represent a subtraction of one value from each of the rhythmic units of *e*.

Ex. 4-27

Asymmetrical diminutions, as vital a part of Messiaen's rhythmic credo as irregular augmentations, reduce the unit values of rhythmic groups in random and unpatterned ways, as illustrated in Ex. 4-28.

Ex. 4-28

Messiaen's nonretrogradable rhythms form patterns whose retrograde in totality is identical to the original sequence of durations (Ex. 4-29*a* and *b*). A retrogradable rhythm, on the other hand, is any pattern whose reverse order does not duplicate the initial sequential outlining of note values (*c* and *d*). The former technique constitutes an integral part of Messiaen's handling of the rhythmic parameter in his music. Also greatly favored by him are palindrome rhythms; they are retrogradable only in that the durational *segments* making up the rhythmic pattern may be reversed without duplicating the original sequence of note values (*e* and *f*).

Ex. 4-29

In his *Messe de la Pentacôte* for organ, Messiaen utilized what he termed "durées chromatiques." In these series of note durations, each member is formed by adding to or subtracting from the previous member one time unit of a constant value. The durational segments must contain at least one time unit; the maximum number allowed is arbitrarily chosen. Ex. 4-30 is a passage from the work wherein the left-hand manual part regularly subtracts one ♪ note from each durational group, from twenty-three down to one; at the same time the pedal part progressively adds one ♪ note to each unit, from four up to twenty-five (with a single interruption of the sequence).

Ex. 4-30. Olivier Messiaen: "Le vent de l'Esprit," from *Messe de la Pentacôte*, p.22

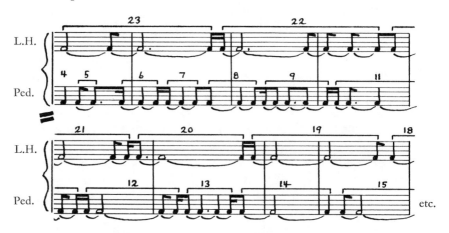

Messiaen's "durational scale" was carried to an extreme in the *Chronochromie (Color of Time)* of 1960. Here the composer made use of thirty-two time values, ranging from a ♪ note to a 𝅝 note, the latter incorporating a total of thirty-two ♪ notes. These thirty-two values were then subjected to every conceivable permutation, singly and in combination, producing a dense web of polyrhythmic strands in which no single pattern could be discerned.

Like so many technical devices formulated primarily through intellectual processes, Messiaen's rhythmic ideas in *Chronochromie* operate more successfully in theory than in reality—at least from the aural standpoint. Almost any complexity can be justified to a degree on paper; perceptually, abstract conceptions cannot always be so easily defended. Yet Messiaen's contributions to modern rhythmic conceptuality are of far more than academic significance. Just as we cannot

readily envision the harmonic and orchestrational explorations of
Strauss, Mahler, Scriabin, and Schoenberg without the previous
enlightenments of Wagner, so we cannot imagine the complex rhythmic
constructs of Boulez, Stockhausen, Carter, Babbitt, or Wuorinen
without the impetus furnished by Messiaen's experimentations and
codifications within the realm of contemporary rhythmic thought.

It is also Olivier Messiaen to whom today's composers are in-
debted for the concept of serialized rhythmic organization. First hinted
at in his extensive treatise of 1944, *La technique de mon langage musical*,
and later demonstrated in *Cantéyodayâ* for piano solo (1948), the concept
was detailed the following year in *Modes de valeurs et d'intensités*. A scale of
twelve durations was applied to the sequent pitches of a twelve-tone
row, beginning with the shortest value (a ♪ note) and extending to the
longest (a ♩. note). Thus the duration of the second pitch in Messiaen's
row is the value of two ♪ notes, or a ♪ note; the rhythmic value of the
third note is the sum of three ♪ notes (♪.)—and so on to the final
pitch of the series, which has the total value of twelve ♪ notes (♩.)
(Ex. 4-31).

Ex. 4-31. Olivier Messiaen: from *Modes de valeurs et d'intensités*

Because a maximum of only twelve different durations would
prove insufficient in any compositional context, Messiaen enlarged his
durational scale to a total of twenty-four individual units. This he
accomplished by initially adding a ♪-note value to the twelfth member
of the series, yielding ♩.. (or ♩.♪) for the thirteenth. Adding a ♪ note
to this latter value produces a ♩ note and represents number fourteen
in the rhythmic order. Each subsequent value was then constructed in
the same manner so that the twenty-fourth, and ultimate, value was
represented by a 𝅝. note.

Both the pitch series and accompanying scale of durations from
Messiaen's pioneering work were appropriated by Pierre Boulez for
the organization of his 1952 *Structures (I)* for two pianos. The opening
measures of the work are remarkable on several counts: first, Boulez
simultaneously exposes both the prime (in Piano I) and the inversion (in

Piano II) of the row (Ex. 4-32*a*). Next, to these two versions of the basic series Boulez applies a rhythmic scheme derived from the durational retrograde (12 to 1). The sequence of durations in Piano I is: 12–11–9–10–3–6–7–1–2–8–4–5; that in Piano II is: 5–8–6–4–3–9–2–1–7–11–10–12. (Compare with Messiaen's original durational series shown in Ex. 4-31.)

Not shown here, but equally vital to the composer's compositional premise, are the dynamics and articulations applied to each pitch and formulated according to serialized principles.

Mathematically minded composers, theorists, and performers may be intrigued by the vertical relationships of the dual rhythmic schemes in Ex. 4-32*a*, juxtaposed on a 1:1 basis (4-32*b*). In actuality, of course, the two durational permutations are not thus synchronized.

Ex. 4-32. Pierre Boulez: *Structures* (*I*), p.1

a.

b.

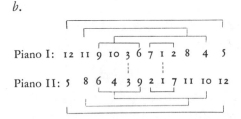

Concurrently with Boulez's work on *Structures*, his German peer Karlheinz Stockhausen was applying the concept of total serialization to his *Kreuzspiel* of 1951 and to "*Kontra-Punkte*" (1953). Each note of the composer's tone rows in each work was subjected to rigorous quadri-dimensional permutation: pitch, duration, intensity, and timbre. This compositional approach has since shaped the structure and contents of many a dodecaphonic work, rhythm being not the least of the parameters so controlled. In fact, as Ernst Krenek has reminded us, because the element of time can be measured and manipulated with as much precision as that of pitch, the serialization of rhythm has had the most consequential and far-reaching influence on the tone-row music of our time.

A later development in the area of serially organized music is Milton Babbitt's "time-point" system, in which interval size in the row forms is equated with duration on a 1:1 basis. Taking the ♬ note as the arbitrarily smallest time unit, this becomes the equivalent of the smallest interval within the duodecuple system, the minor second. The next larger interval, the major second, would then be represented by two ♬'s, or an ♪ note. Each increment in interval size is therefore expressed by an analogically longer durational value. The largest interval in our system of twelve tones is the major seventh (or diminished octave); its rhythmic equivalent in the time-point system would be the total of eleven ♬ notes, or ♩ ♪..

For purposes of simple illustration we borrow the Messiaen-Boulez tone row of Exs. 4-31 and 4-32 and apply to it a durational scheme according to the time-point principle (Ex. 4-33a). Considered compositionally rather than merely theoretically, the sequence of note durations might appear as at *b*. Were intervallic inversions to be used in the initial row order (a minor second becoming a major seventh, for instance), the rhythmic plan would be accordingly altered, as demonstrated at *c*.

It will be noted that the prime inversion of the row would command the same durational series as the original, the intervallic relationships being identical. Likewise the retrograde forms of both prime and inversion would require a similar durational sequence unless interval inversions were liberally employed. It would then follow that all transpositions of the four basic row forms would be alike, theoretically, in their rhythmic structures; realistically, no composer would allow this to happen but would insure flexibility and contrast by inverting intervals where necessary and by liberally using such common dodecaphonic devices as row interruption and transferral of row forms from one voice to another.

Ernst Krenek, in his *Sestina* of 1957, used a somewhat parallel method of deriving and manipulating time values from the basic

Ex. 4-33

tone-row forms. The composer first divided his work into a certain number of equal time segments; each was then assigned as many different pitches from the row as the first interval outlined contained half steps. This being a major third (four half steps) the initial time segment contains the first four notes of the composer's set. Krenek explains how the individual note durations were established: "[They] are determined by dividing the number of the units by the sum of as many figures of the intervallic series as the number of tones contained in the segment indicates. The quotient thus obtained is then multiplied by the interval number and the result is the duration of the individual tone (the interval series is 4–3–1–6–2–etc.). The first segment is thus four units. The sum of the first four numbers in the series is 14. Four divided by 14 is $\frac{2}{7}$. The durations of the tones are $\frac{8}{7}$, $\frac{6}{7}$, $\frac{2}{7}$, and $\frac{12}{7}$ of one-fourth of the entire segment."[5] Each succeeding segment in Krenek's composition is treated similarly, the rhythmic framework of the entire piece thus becoming one huge mathematical construct. It is significant that even Krenek himself senses the dangers inherent in such a scientific and essentially cold-blooded approach to composition. "The fact is," he states, "that the numbers arrived at through procedures of the type described detach themselves from the musical elements of their origin and become objects of arithmetic operations, the results

5. Ernst Krenek, "Serialism," in *Dictionary of Contemporary Music*, ed. John Vinton (New York: E. P. Dutton & Co., Inc., 1974), pp.670–74.

MODERN METRICAL CONCEPTS AND THEIR NOTATIONS 115

of which are then reapplied to the musical material. The composer may believe that the descendence of the numbers from the tone row makes the music orderly and artistically meaningful. But this is based more on mystique than on demonstrable fact."

All the system proposals so far discussed, designed both for the expansion of rhythmic concepts and for the improvement of rhythmic notation in twentieth-century music, have been firmly based on the precepts of metrical organization. Even Messiaen's theories of duration, though they generally lie outside conventional meter and time signatures, are based on the hierarchical relativity of traditional note values. But current rhythmic conceptuality and practice also draws heavily on a durational relativity that is not geared to traditional note distinctions. Composers now frequently grade their pitch durations into three broad categories: short, medium, and long—without necessarily specifying precise time lengths. To this end they make use of notehead forms that do not show mathematical relationships, but only approximate ratios:

short = ● or ♪   medium = ♪ or ♩   long = ○ or □

Frequently timings are indicated within each of the categories, exact or approximate, but again without basing relative durations on arithmetical notehead distinctions, as in orthochronic notation:

$$\text{♪} = \tfrac{1}{2}\text{-}1''\qquad\qquad \text{♩} = 1\text{-}2''\qquad\qquad \text{○} = 2\text{-}4''$$

The principal difficulty with both of the approaches illustrated lies not with the fundamental concept but with the conspicuous absence of agreement among practicing composers as to the symbology most appropriate to these loosely relative note durations. The note symbols shown represent only a very few out of those used by today's composers for nonmetrical rhythmic delineation; they are archetypal but not standardized.

A related conceptual technique is that by which the composer specifies a free or highly variable durational scheme, allowing performers to adjust both tempo and rhythm according to their spontaneous reactions. For note groups to be played as fast as possible, a specification that allows for considerable latitude, depending upon the abilities of the individual performer and the nature of the instrument played, a grace-note format is quite generally favored (Ex. 4-34a). For passages of variable rhythmic durations not based on metrical relationships, the composer usually resorts to irregular note spacing (b) or to the use of nonconformist symbols that require careful explication (c).

Ex. 4-34

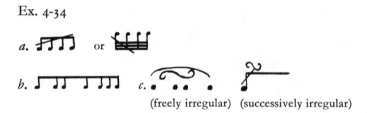

a. ♫♫♩ or ♫♫♩

b. ♩ ♫ ♩ ♫ *c.* • ‿ • • •   ♪

(freely irregular)   (successively irregular)

Closely related to the concept of variable tempo is the notational device by which rubato is given graphic representation (Ex. 4-35). For *accelerando* the beams over a group of notes are fanned out from one to two or more (*a*), while for *ritardando* they are drawn in from two or more beams to a single ligature (*b*). Both changes in pace are intended to be nonmetrical and hence only approximate in durational relativity. Because these pictorial manifestations of *accelerando* and *ritardando* are so visually effective, however, many composers utilize them in metrically organized music in order to obviate excessively complicated and cluttered rhythmical distinctions.

Ex. 4-35

a. ♩ ♩ ♩ ♩ ♪♪♪   *b.* ♫♫♫ ♩ ♩ ♩

A new symbology, concomitant with those previously mentioned, has been applied to holds and pauses, sometimes specific as to length (Ex. 4-36*a*) and sometimes indeterminate (*b*). Although the symbols used are clearly based on the traditional fermata sign and, generally speaking, there is a marked difference between the symbols utilized for durational extremes, the principal difficulty inherent in the system is illustrated by the series of signs advocated by Stockhausen and by Serge Garant. In Stockhausen's case the square fermata sign indicates the longest duration in his series; in Garant's list, to the contrary, it means a short pause. This notational dichotomy can be multiplied many times over in comparing score after score in which these and other visually related pause and hold signs appear. Unless composers can agree on the most logical order of their fermata-based symbols, whether in a nonmetrical context or otherwise, only confusion and frustration for the performer can result.

The most prevalent and influential development in nonmetrical notation today is without a doubt that termed "proportionate" (analog, or time) notation. Resulting from certain experiments made by

Ex. 4-36

a. Karlheinz Stockhausen: *Refrain*

⊓ = ca. 4,0″
⌢ = ca. 2,5″
Λ = ca. 1,5″
V = ca. 1,0″
꒰ = ca. 0,5″

b. Serge Garant: *Pièce pour Piano no. 2*

⊡ = very long pause
⌢ = long pause
Λ = medium pause
⊓ = short pause
V = very short pause

the American composer Earle Brown in 1952, time notation was subsequently adopted by many international composers of widely divergent musical styles. The explicit premise of the system is simple: to equate durational length with horizontal space (Ex. 4-37*a*). Indeed, one might echo the words of Gurnemanz to the young Parsifal in Act I of Wagner's opera: "... zum Raum wird hier die Zeit" (here time is one with space).

Proportionate notation thus substitutes a geometric for a symbolistic representation of rhythm and duration. Just as four seconds of clock time require a correspondingly longer interval than does one second, so a note or event requiring four "beats" or counting units will occupy four times as much linear space as a note of one tactus. Scores utilizing the principle of analog notation usually have their pages or systems divided into arbitrarily chosen units of seconds, sometimes marked off in inches or centimeters (see Ex. 4-38).

Two principal methods are currently in use for delineating individual note or chord time-length with proportional, or optical, notation. One method extends the notehead proper to designate its total time span (Ex. 4-37*b* and *c*, and see also Ex. 4-39); the other extends a single ligature from the stemmed note or sonority to the point in space of durational termination (Ex. 4-37*d*, and see Ex. 4-38). There are, however, seemingly as many calligraphic variants of these two basic formats as there are composers utilizing the technique. In an exhaustive survey made by this writer of twentieth-century notation in all its aspects, some sixty-eight different versions of the dual methods just described were observed and codified.[6] There is, one thinks, little justification for such a plethora of formats to indicate a single musical parameter—analogical duration in time on the score page.

Ex. 4-37

Optically notated music is a viable alternative to metrically conceived, hypercomplex, and minutely designated rhythmic schemata, found in such scores as Elliott Carter's *Double Concerto*, or *Structures* by Boulez (Ex. 4-32). The technique is a valid means of freeing pulse, tactus, and measured rhythmic progress from the straitjacket of conventional notation, with its restrictive reliance on time signatures, barlines, and regularly recurring units of time—not to mention irrational groupings that still must relate to explicit meters and their obligatory barlines and to measurable units of time within those barlines.

It is significant that the principle of proportionate note spacing is now frequently applied to compositions that are conventionally metered or whose "measures" are uniform in horizontal space, which amounts to the same thing as indicating an unchanging time signature. Individual notes within such measures, however, are not related to one another

6. Gardner Read, *Twentieth-Century Notation*. Ms., 1971. A microfilm of the manuscript is included in the Index of New Musical Notation, Library of the Performing Arts, Lincoln Center, New York, N.Y.

Ex. 4-38. Gardner Read: *Sonoric Fantasia no. 3*, p.24. © 1972 by
Seesaw Music Corporation, New York. Reproduced by permission.

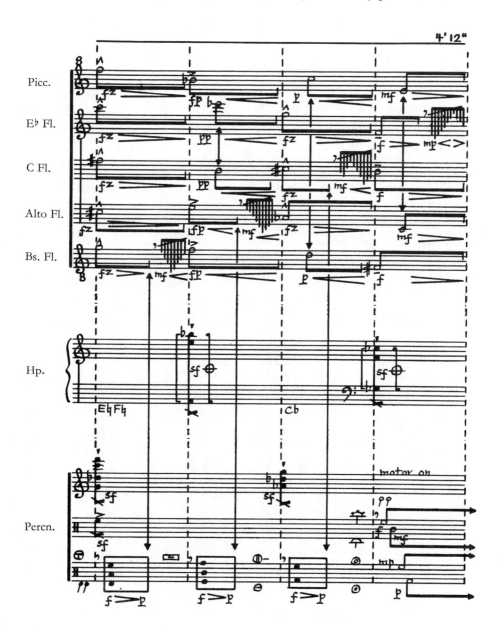

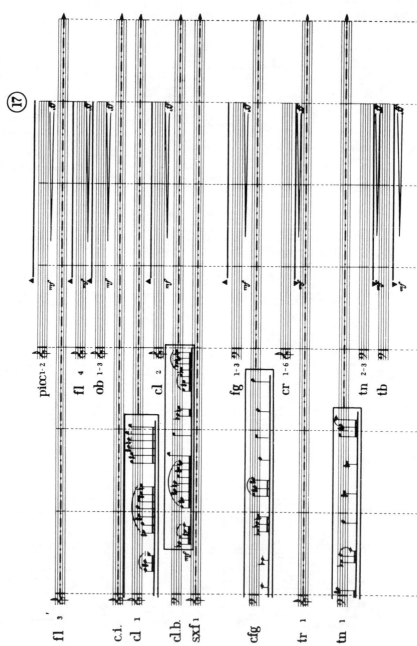

Ex. 4-39. Krzystof Penderecki: *De Natura Sonoris* (I), p.24. © 1967 by Moeck Verlag, Celle FRG. Used with permission. All rights reserved.

Ex. 4-40. Gunther Schuller: *American Triptych*, p.24. © 1966 by Associated
Music Publishers, Inc. Used by permission.

with mathematical exactness as they must be in metrical music. Rather, the notes are placed at points in linear space corresponding to approximate points in time within the encompassing barlines. The performers thus react to the notes according to their visual positions. In addition, there are no longer temporal distinctions in notehead color (whether solid or open), nor do flags and beams have other than relative significance (as in Ex. 4-38).

A brief excerpt taken from Krzystof Penderecki's early *De Natura Sonoris* (*I*) (Ex. 4-39) clearly demonstrates the analogical approach to rhythmic notation. Additionally, the excerpt illustrates yet another aspect of aleatoric notation—namely, that commonly referred to as "frame" notation. The sequence of pitches enclosed in boxes or frames is to be repeated for a designated length of time, usually in random order and with aperiodic rhythms.

Many contemporary scores now combine or alternate metrical and proportionate notation, such as Gunther Schuller's *American Triptych*, from which a brief passage is excerpted in Ex. 4-40. Thus a precise and usually complex rhythmic edifice is alternated with or even superimposed upon a fluid, aperiodic durational texture. Far from being mutually incompatible, the two systems can—and do—coexist on the best of terms.

Of all the modern notational techniques discussed here, time notation promises to have the greatest durability. Optically designed notation is clearly a conceptual idea whose time had arrived by mid-century. It is, *inter alia*, the best method by which the theory of durational probability may be transferred to the science of musical symbology. If for no other reason, proportionate notation is obviously destined to assume the same strategic position in late twentieth-century compositional techniques as the rhythmic modes did in the music of the thirteenth and fourteenth centuries. Time notation would thus seem to be the *Ars nova* of modern times. It may prove to be the one compositional technique above all others that will influence music designed for the human performer during the next century.

5

Polymetric Notation

Implicit Polymeters

Now that the specialized techniques and related notational procedures of additive, mixed, fractional, and decimal meters have been
discussed and illuminated by means of copious examples, we are
concerned here with the symbological techniques of simultaneous
time signatures, more usually referred to as polymeters. Conceptually,
polymeters represent one of the more advanced manifestations of
modern rhythmic practice. When combined with the technique of
simultaneous tempi, polymeters can extend the boundaries of metrical
and rhythmic structure almost to the vanishing point. Such a con-
ceptualization unmistakably approaches the realm of analogical rhythm
and time notation (see, for instance, Ex. 5-63). Nonetheless, when
employed discriminatively polymeters can serve as powerful psychological agents in the composer's technical repository. By means of the
opposition of two or more conflicting metrical schemata, a rhythmic
autonomy of singular complexity can be achieved. Polymetric designs
are thus direct parallels to polytonal harmonic fabrics, both techniques
creating unity in contrast and agreement through opposition.

A polymetric ambience may be achieved in two ways: by implication, and in actuality. Multiple time signatures may be implied within
a single all-inclusive meter by means of consistent cross-accenting or
patterned irregular phrasing in one or more musical strands of a given
composition. Polymeters may also, of course, be created by the
employment of several differing time signatures used concurrently.

Although implicit polymeters can occasionally be located in certain
Baroque, Classical, and both early and late Romantic scores, it was not
until the present century that the technique became a prominent feature
of developing rhythmic concepts. Curt Sachs[1] has pointed out that

1. *Rhythm and Tempo*, p.289.

123

an early example of implied simultaneous time signatures occurs in the
Et Resurrexit section of Bach's *B-minor Mass* (Ex. 5-1). It is extremely
doubtful, however, that Bach consciously thought of a polymetric
concurrence here; more likely he considered the bass line as merely
shifting its primary accent ahead by one beat in each successive measure,
as the passage in question quickly regains the indisputable triple pattern
established throughout the section as a whole. Furthermore, polymeters—whether implicit or actual—were basically inimical to the spirit
of Baroque expression and to the accepted norms of rhythmic delineation in that music; hence dual signatures find no place in the compositions of Bach and his contemporaries.

Ex. 5-1. Johann Sebastian Bach: *B-minor Mass*, p.143

In the present century, however, the concurrent use of differing
time signatures, implied or actual, is a vital part of rhythmic organization. The first movement, *Prélude à la nuit*, of Maurice Ravel's *Rapsodie
espagnole*, for instance, exhibits a clear and sustained implicit polymetric scheme (Ex. 5-2). From first to almost last measure, with but
occasional momentary interruptions, a steady four-note descending
scale figure is set against the underlying and unequivocal three beats of
the stated time signature. This is the equivalent of notating $\frac{2}{4}$ against $\frac{3}{4}$,
with equal $\downarrow$ notes.

Would Ravel's polyrhythmic idea have been more clearly expressed
had he used two time signatures? Perhaps not, mainly because of the

relative simplicity of the opposing rhythmic schemes and the fact that
the composer was able to beam the four-note groups, crossing barlines
every two measures, as visual confirmation of that opposition.

Ex. 5-2. Maurice Ravel: *Rapsodie espagnole*, p.1

A nearly identical pattern of repeated four-♪-note groups within a
basic ¾ meter is to be found near the end of Ralph Vaughan Williams's
Pastoral Symphony (p.100 of the study score). The implicit ²⁄₄ meter here
is suggested not so much by beamings as by the sequential pattern of
pitch repetitions and accompanying bowing slurs in the string instruments entrusted with the quadruple note cell.

A similar, and constantly recurring, pattern of four ♪ notes is
spread over a number of ⁹⁄₈ measures in Stravinsky's *Le Sacre du Prin-*
temps, suggesting ⁴⁄₈ against ⁹⁄₈, with ♪ note equalling ♪ note (see Ex.
5-3*a*). The composer, however, does not beam together the groups of
four ♪ notes, as would be expected, but relies instead on accents to
show the irregular rhythmic divisions of each measure. On the other
hand, Stravinsky does beam consistently a figure of four ♪ notes in a ⁵⁄₈
meter toward the close of *Petrouchka*, the unified group thus bisecting
the barlines every two measures (Ex. 5-3*b*).

Ex. 5-3

a. Igor Stravinsky: *Le Sacre du Printemps*, p.30

b. Igor Stravinsky: *Petrouchka*, p.146

A more recent example is George Rochberg's *Night Music*, in which there is a nineteen-page passage containing a dual ostinato in harp and violins in two implicit and differing meters. Midway through the section the composer superimposes yet another metric scheme, made more explicit by virtue of dotted barlines in the part affected. Thus, four simultaneous meters are in momentary operation, two of them explicit and two implicit, as shown in Ex. 5-4.

Ex. 5-4. George Rochberg: *Night Music*, pp.17, 22

Implied polymetrical ostinati of both fewer and more rhythmic (counting) units are naturally feasible; they frequently characterize extended passages in scores of the twentieth century (Ex. 5-5). The polymetric patterns in 5-5*a, c, e, f,* and *g* are made manifest by beamings over the barlines; in *b* and *d* they are indicated by other means.

Ex. 5-5

a. Alban Berg: *Drei Orchesterstücke,* p.77

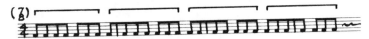

b. Leonard Bernstein: *The Age of Anxiety,* p.73

c. Leonard Bernstein: *"West Side Story" Symphonic Dances,* p.41

d. Leonard Bernstein: Ibid., p.17

e. Aaron Copland: *First Symphony*, p.38

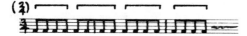

f. Edward Elgar: *Symphony no. 2*, p.90

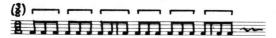

g. Michael Tippett: *Symphony no. 2*, p.89

The examples discussed thus far have all been based on the conjunction of implicit polymetric patterns in simple duple or triple time. As an example of implied polymeters operating within an irregular (but here unspecified) time signature, the excerpt from one of Olivier Messiaen's organ compositions is both intriguing and significant (Ex. 5-6). The dual patterns shown continue for a total of nine measures, with the right-hand (upper) part always staying within the limitation of an implied $\frac{10}{16}$ (or $\frac{5}{8}$) measure, while the lower part consistently subtracts one ♪ note from each measure length as it progresses to the end of the nine measures. Although nine ♪ notes thus constitute the part's metrical framework, they do not represent compound time. In simplified notation the actual pattern is

♪ ♫♫ ♫, and not ♫ ♫♫ ♫.

Ex. 5-6. Olivier Messiaen: *Le Verbe*, from *La Nativité du Seigneur*, p.2

Implicit polymeters can also operate quite effectively within a context of changing time signatures. For example: a four-♪-note ostinato figure enlivening the final pages of Stravinsky's *Dumbarton Oaks* Concerto (beginning at no. 83) cuts across numerous changes of signature, implying a constant $\frac{2}{4}$ ($\frac{4}{8}$) over alternating measures of $\frac{3}{4}$, $\frac{2}{4}$, and $\frac{4}{4}$ (Ex. 5-7). And an almost identical ostinato occurs in *L'Histoire du Soldat* (in Scenes 1 and 3), where the doublebass has a four-note figure of ♪'s in $\frac{2}{4}$, continuing the pattern inflexibly through subsequent changes of meter to $\frac{3}{8}$, $\frac{5}{8}$, and $\frac{3}{4}$.

The device of maintaining a never-varying rhythmic ostinato regardless of intervening meter changes is rather an *idée fixe* in Stravinsky's conceptual handling of rhythm. In *Chant du Rossignol* there is a three-note figure of ♪'s that goes its independent way irrespective of frequent meter changes (Ex. 5-8). It is interesting to note that when both rhythmic parts commonly share a $\frac{3}{8}$ time signature, their respective and individual stresses come at different points within the measure, thus preserving a marked metrical autonomy.

Yet another occurrence of implied polymeter that continues without change throughout a number of measures of variable meter comes from the cantata *Abraham and Isaac* (Ex. 5-9). This passage is rather curiously notated because Stravinsky chose to express an implicit $\frac{3}{16}$ as an ♪ note tied to a ♪ note (or vice versa), rather than using the more conventional single-note value (♪.) when possible.

A far more complex instance of implied polymetricality appears in *L'Histoire du Soldat*, where, at one particular point, four different implicit meters operate simultaneously within a framework of constantly changing time signatures (Ex. 5-10). Furthermore, only one of these four metrical patterns adheres to the underlying pulsation of the stated meter; the others are in opposition not only to each other but also to the explicit and variable signatures. This manner of metrical interweaving is typical of Stravinsky's abstraction of rhythmic independence, and the technique informs many another passage in this and others of his works.

Not always, of course, can a notator conveniently rely on beaming patterns to convey visually an implicit polymetric procedure, as demonstrated in the several Stravinsky compositions just cited. In Maurice Ravel's *L'Enfant et les sortilèges*, for instance, a four-against-three metrical pattern must be written in ♩ notes against ♩· notes in a $\frac{3}{4}$ meter, illustrated in Ex. 5-11. The use of these note values precludes ligatures, with which the opposing metric scheme might be visually confirmed, as when ♪'s and smaller values are present. Furthermore, the bowing slurs under the ♩-note phrases conform to the normal rhythmic stresses of the $\frac{3}{4}$ signature, one slur to each measure. Without irregular accentuations, only the sequence of recurring pitches makes manifest the implicit polymetric schemata.

Another prolonged sequence of a ♩-note figure reveals the implied polymetric design at work in the initial movement of Stravinsky's *Symphony in Three Movements* (Ex. 5-12). Without the tangible benefits of beamings, brackets, or clearly notated accentual patterns, the implicit $\frac{3}{4}$

Ex. 5-7. Igor Stravinsky: *Dumbarton Oaks* Concerto, p.41

Ex. 5-8. Igor Stravinsky: *Chant du Rossignol*, p.22

Ex. 5-9. Igor Stravinsky: *Abraham and Isaac*, p.6

Ex. 5-10. Igor Stravinsky: *L'Histoire du Soldat*, p.35

Ex. 5-11. Maurice Ravel: *L'Enfant et les sortilèges*, p.162

of the bass line is evidenced only by the inflexible recurrence of the three-note melodic figure. Like so many of Stravinsky's bass ostinati, the figure here continues without change through several successive time signatures, never yielding its rhythmic autonomy.

Ex. 5-12. Igor Stravinsky: *Symphony in Three Movements*, p.8

A similarly implicit $\frac{3}{4}$ is imposed upon a basic $\frac{4}{4}$ meter in Aaron Copland's ballet suite *Billy the Kid* (pp.14–17 of the study score), but here it is made visually evident by virtue of dotted barlines placed after each third beat of the conflicting pattern. (Compare with the Rochberg citation in Ex. 5-4.)

The establishment of implicit polymeters obviously may affect the rhythmic progress of several compositional parts, and it may do so in completely different manners, all within an expressed time signature that is in evident opposition to those parts. A clear example of this occurs in Copland's early *Dance Symphony*: here a four-note figure in even ♪ notes and a three-note figure comprising two ♪'s and an ♩ note are superimposed upon a basic $\frac{3}{8}$ meter. Both patterns, therefore, reflect an implicit $\frac{2}{8}$ against $\frac{3}{8}$, but their primary accents do not coincide, as demonstrated in Ex. 5-13. A few score pages later there is a complex juxtaposition of three polymetrical patterns, all accommodated within the basic signature of $\frac{3}{8}$. The composer's metrical solution of the uppermost part of Ex. 5-14 was included on a cue-staff for the benefit of the conductor. This solution, however, is anything but obvious if one interprets the rhythmic design by the recurring accentuations. Copland's first measure of implied $\frac{5}{8}$ is syncopated in relation to the primary beat of the underlying $\frac{3}{8}$, whereas the second is not. A more consistent polymetrical notation is shown on the uppermost staff in parentheses, although admittedly it is conspicuously at odds with Copland's evident intent. It should be obvious, however, that whichever implied metrical pattern one chooses to consider, the polyrhythmic totality will be one of singular tension and complexity.

We find an even more extensive assortment of implicit meters in the third section, *In the Night*, of Charles Ives's *A Set of Pieces*: within the

Ex. 5-13. Aaron Copland: *Dance Symphony*, p.55

Ex. 5-14. Ibid., p.64

overall time signature of $\frac{3}{4}$, one instrumental group establishes a steady pattern of four ♩ notes (or an implicit $\frac{4}{4}$) whose internal phrasings are in four groups of three notes and four of two (Ex. 5-15). At the same time another instrumental voice sharing the full measure quadruplet outlines a corresponding $\frac{12}{16}$–$\frac{8}{16}$ rhythmic pattern. Yet another group of instruments just as unequivocally establishes a steady $\frac{3}{16}$ figure, while still another group proceeds with an undeviating $\frac{2}{4}$ design. Thus, not one of the four different operational patterns observes the basic metrical framework of $\frac{3}{4}$. The passage quoted is typical of Ives's freewheeling approach to polyrhythm—a "devil take the hindmost" philosophy of composition and related performance technicalities.

A particularly effective instance of implicit metric duality occurs in the final movement of Arthur Honegger's *Symphony no. 2* (Ex. 5-16). Within the stated time signature of $\frac{6}{8}$, which is maintained by the lower strings, the two violin sections each progress in an unmistakable $\frac{5}{8}$ pulsation, but their respective accentual patterns do not coincide. Eventually the conflicting $\frac{5}{8}$ patterns are reabsorbed into the movement's dominant meter.

Somewhat milder in its duality is a passage in Stravinsky's early opera *Le Rossignol*: without altering or destroying the basic triple

Ex. 5-15. Charles Ives: *A Set of Pieces*, p.20

Ex. 5-16. Arthur Honegger: *Symphony no. 2*, p.39

pulsation expressed by the $\frac{3}{8}$ time signature, the composer merely shifts his primary accent in one instrumental voice to mid-measure so that a subtle and continual syncopation is created (Ex. 5-17).

Ex. 5-17. Igor Stravinsky: *Le Rossignol*, p.62

Hemiola and sesquialtera are both venerable rhythmic devices that still play a role in the establishment of implicit polymeters. Hemiola—the technique of combining or alternating simple and compound rhythmic grouping within a single basic meter—has been extensively exploited by twentieth-century composers. An excellent, and familiar, example is demonstrated at the outset of the slow movement to Ravel's *Piano Concerto in G*: here the left hand of the solo piano part has an extended chordal ostinato figure of six ♪ notes within the ¾ meter, but phrased in two groups of three (Ex. 5-18). The accompanying ostinato is thus actually in an implicit ⅜, two measures of which equal one measure of the unequivocal ¾ in the right-hand melodic voice.[2] Owing to the uniform stresses in the left-hand part the pulsation is more truly felt as two groups of three ♪ notes rather than one unified group of six (to conform to ⁶⁄₈, or compound time against simple time).

Ex. 5-18. Maurice Ravel: *Piano Concerto in G*, p.49

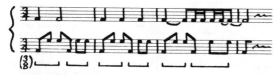

Implied polymetrical schemata have frequently been used imitatively in twentieth-century compositions. In the initial movement of Arnold Schoenberg's *Five Pieces for Orchestra*, measures 64–72, a three-note figure in ♪ notes within a time signature of ⁴⁄₈ is canonically displaced by one ♪ note in each of three instrumental lines (Ex. 5-19a). The rhythmic result is equivalent to writing all three lines in ⅜, with each part commencing on a different beat.

Implicit and actual polymeters soon join forces in this same passage: superimposed on the imitative scheme illustrated in *a* is yet another canonic design in ⅜ (*b*). The most intriguing aspect of the entire rhythmic construct is that the phrasing patterns in the triple meters are duple, while those in the duple meters are triple—a curious reversal of the normal, and expected, accentuations. Later in the same movement (measures 91–94) a four-note figure in ♪'s is similarly imitated between four separate instrumental parts (*c*). Here the metrical imitation adheres to the stated time signature of ⁴⁄₈, but each part commences its imitation one ♪ note later in the measure.

Imitation within an implicit polymetric fabric is an unmistakable hallmark of the compositional techniques of both Schoenberg and Berg. In particular, the opera *Lulu* is replete with passages containing imitative sequences of rhythmic groups whose accentuations and durations are in clear opposition to the stated time signatures. To cite one especially complex example: Berg has here coupled two polyrhythmic figures, each of which is treated imitatively and each of which

---

2. In Ildebrando Pizzetti's *Concerto del'Estate* a similar implicit metrical juxtaposition is expressed by the time signature of ⅜ × 2 = ¾.

Ex. 5-19. Arnold Schoenberg: *Five Pieces for Orchestra*

a. p.9

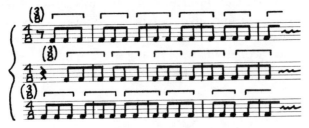

b. p.9

c. p.13

operates within a different division of the basic $\frac{3}{4}$ time units (Ex. 5-20). One figure is in steady ♪ notes, but phrased in groups of five, implying a $\frac{5}{16}$ signature. Against this scheme is set a figure in ♪-note triplets, which suggests simultaneous compound time, or $\frac{9}{8}$ (sesquialtera). The triplets, however, are phrased in grouplets of four rather than three notes, as would normally be the case. Simple and compound time are thus juxtaposed, creating cross-rhythm, but the texture is further complicated by the irregular imitative phrasings in both rhythmic patterns.

Ex. 5-20. Alban Berg: *Lulu* Suite, p.84

Another closely related instance of implied polymetric imitation is revealed in the first of the *Altenberg Lieder*, op. 4: on page one a five-note ostinato figure in ♪ notes in $\frac{4}{8}$ meter is consistently beamed over the barlines, clearly establishing a pattern of $\frac{5}{8}$, and exactly imitated one ♪ note later in another instrumental part. Additional occurrences of this type of imitative metrical texture may easily be located in other scores of both Berg and Schoenberg, especially in the latter's *Variations for Orchestra* and *Violin Concerto*.

It is curious that, in spite of their almost inordinate fondness for rhythmical and metrical cross-fertilization, neither Berg nor Schoenberg extensively indulged in the notation of explicit polymeters; in fact, Berg conspicuously shunned the device of simultaneous time signatures, even when their presence might have been of considerable aid to performers. It is true that Schoenberg occasionally used concurrent simple and compound meters, such as the combined $\frac{12}{8}$ and $\frac{4}{4}$ signatures of the opening theme of the *Variations for Orchestra*. But Schoenberg, like Berg, often bypassed even this common practice when its use might have been interpretively helpful. A clear case in point occurs at the beginning of the second movement of the *Violin Concerto*, where the composer resorts to repeated and notationally cumbersome triplets in simple time rather than altering his time signature to compound meter.

In Schoenberg's defense one must mention the rather minor poly-
metric involvements ($\frac{3}{8}$ over $\frac{2}{4}$ and $\frac{4}{8}$) in the first of the *Five Pieces for
Orchestra* and in the op. 7 string quartet ($\frac{3}{4}$ over $\frac{2}{4}$). These isolated
instances, however, represent Schoenberg's most evident reliance on
simultaneous differing meters and are not typical of his customary
rhythmic predilections. Among the Viennese triumvirate it remained
for Anton Webern to exploit the technique of actual polymetricality
to the extent of using dual signatures throughout an entire movement
of a work. (See Ex. 5-32.) Webern's *raison d'être*, however, was strictly
conditioned by the work's contrapuntal premise, not by any desire for
extraneous rhythmic effect for its own sake.

Implicit polymetric imitation is a prominent feature of the second
movement of Béla Bartók's *Music for Strings, Percussion and Celesta*. (The
passage cited is also polyharmonic, the composer having hetero-
phonically juxtaposed two dominant-ninth chords whose roots are a
tritone apart.) Within a basic meter of $\frac{2}{4}$ Bartók combines three versions
of $\frac{5}{8}$, each delayed by one ♪ note, as shown on the second, third, and
fourth lines of Ex. 5-21. Oddly enough, Bartók did not avail himself
of the obvious device of trans-barline beamings—a notational technique
that characterizes many of his other polyrhythmic compositions.
Neither does he use brackets, dotted barlines, accent marks, or any
other indicia to pinpoint the imitative patterns, all of which are in
opposition to the actual time signature. To the analytical eye, then, only
the sequential designs of the pitches indicate the polymetrical scheme
in operation. Furthermore, the syncopated patterns in the piano and
first string orchestra parts (top line of the example) only occasionally
agree with the basic signature in regard to primary stress. The entire
passage, therefore, is at constant odds with the stated $\frac{2}{4}$ meter, the
regularly spaced barlines being thus deprived of their traditional
function as indicators of regular and patterned stress.

Ex. 5-21. Béla Bartók: *Music for Strings, Percussion and Celesta*, p.28

On the other hand, not only are essential trans-barline ligatures present in the short quotation from Bartók's fifth string quartet (Ex. 5-22), but the four imitative patterns in this implicit polymetric passage basically agree with the stated meter of $\frac{2}{4}$, even though two of the parts commence their contrapuntal play on displaced beats within the measure. A feeling of one $\frac{4}{4}$ measure rather than two $\frac{2}{4}$ measures in each of the four string parts is established by Bartók's phrasings (bowing slurs).

Ex. 5-22. Béla Bartók: *String Quartet no. 5*, p.71

Though it would appear to be a contradiction in terms, it is possible to indicate implicit polymeters in an explicit manner. Conflicting strata of metrical frameworks can operate in music that is not conventionally organized with stated time signatures, yet is not constructed analogically. A good example of this technique can be seen in the violin and piano sonata of Stefan Wolpe: nearly every page of this work demonstrates the use of non-conterminous barlines between violin and piano parts whose respective measures are devoid of specified meter signatures. The durational lengths of these measures vary constantly, in random sequences, but always with isochronic ♪ notes.[3] The polymetric texture of the music, therefore, exists by implication, yet the notation explicitly outlines the metrical duality of the two instrumental parts.

3. From the Greek *isos* ("equal") and *chronos* ("time"); isochronic thus refers to equal intervals or units of time.

The argument can be reasonably advanced that many, if not all, of the foregoing citations of so-called implicit polymeter should instead be regarded as examples of polyrhythm. The distinction may well be academic, even tenuous; yet the claim can still be made persuasively that when polyrhythm assumes a clear repetitive pattern with undeniable independence in the area of pulsation and stress, metrical rather than merely rhythmical autonomy is conclusively demonstrated. But whether one chooses to regard implied polymeter as only a rather specialized manifestation of polyrhythm or otherwise, the technique remains one of the composer's most potent organizational tools. And it need hardly be said that the notational problems and their ultimate solutions will be largely the same in either instance.

Explicit Polymeters

The notational ambiguities frequently created by extended passages of implicit polymetric design often hinder rather than assist the performer in solving rhythmic complexities. When the compositional premise is one of committed polymetric opposition or contrast, the composer's intent is surely made clearer and more unequivocal by the utilization of simultaneous differing time signatures.

In all the musical excerpts previously discussed, the implied polymetric designs were employed on a somewhat limited basis—not haphazardly, of course, but still on a relatively restricted scale. Thus the composers' reliance on beaming patterns, accentual indicia, and phrasing slurs to show the desired disparity in their rhythmic frameworks usually served as well as could be expected. But other composers, equally committed to advanced rhythmic thought and practice, have deemed these rather cumbersome procedures inadequate. They have found their notational solutions in the device of time-signature duality.

Explicit polymeters are not, of course, unique to contemporary composition; nonetheless, twentieth-century composers have utilized them more extensively than the musical creators of previous periods, the Renaissance included. The enormous expansion of rhythmic concepts in the music of our time—in the Western hemisphere, at least—has inevitably led composers to combine time signatures and polyrhythmic groupings with the same conviction and fluency with which they superimposed different chordal strata to create polyharmony. It would be misleading, however, to infer that polyharmony, polytonality, and polymetric techniques arrived on the musical scene simultaneously. Although polyharmony is indisputably a twentieth-century compositional conceptuality, the concurrent use of differing time signatures appeared, even if sporadically, in the Classical period and very occasionally in late Romantic scores as well.

One of the most frequently cited examples of explicit polymeter in the Classical period occurs in Mozart's opera *Don Giovanni*. In the celebrated ballroom scene (Act I finale), three small orchestras on stage each play a different dance, with correspondingly different time signatures. Orchestra I, together with the vocal parts of Donna Anna, Donna Elvira, and Don Ottavio are in $\frac{3}{4}$; Orchestra II and the vocal lines of Zerlina and the Don himself are in $\frac{2}{4}$, while Orchestra III and the parts for Leporello and Masetto are in $\frac{3}{8}$ (Ex. 5-23*a*).

It might reasonably be argued that Mozart could have achieved the identical polyrhythmic effect more simply by remaining within a common meter for all parts—surely, the $\frac{3}{4}$ of the all-pervasive minuet played by Orchestra I. The $\frac{3}{8}$ waltz in Orchestra III is, after all, merely an alternative manner of notating triplet ♪'s in $\frac{3}{4}$, while the $\frac{2}{4}$ quadrille in Orchestra II could easily be made to fit into $\frac{3}{4}$ by means of displaced accents. Thus, the polyrhythmic scheme of this skillfully meshed passage *might* have been notated by the composer as shown in Ex. 5-23*b*.

Notational simplification, though usually an unarguable asset in clarifying rhythmic complexities, does not invariably serve a composer's true intent, however. In this particular instance a simpler notation would conspicuously miss the point of the dramatic conflict exemplified by the metrical schemata of the three orchestras and seven vocalists, each representing a different musical—and psychological—mood. The polymeters, therefore, represent far more than mere metrical opposition; they signify human conflict as well.[4]

Composed nearly a century later, and notably striking for the creative period in which it was conceived, is the polymetric design at the conclusion of Richard Wagner's *Götterdämmerung* (Ex. 5-24). The simultaneous outlining of three musical ideas is not at all unusual for Wagner, but the concurrent use of two time signatures—and radically different ones—is unique among his operas. Though the juxtaposition

4. Few contemporary performances of the opera scrupulously adhere to Mozart's directive that before playing, Orchestras II and III audibly tune (*accordando*), while Orchestra I carries on with the minuet. Were they always to do so, as the composer intended, an element of fortuitous polytonality would be added to the total musical (and dramatic) effect.

Ex. 5-23. Wolfgang Amadeus Mozart: *Don Giovanni*, Act I, Scene 20, p.194

a.

b.

of various leitmotifs is quite common throughout the entire *Ring* cycle, the device is ordinarily accommodated within a single basic meter. It seems obvious that psychological and dramatic rather than notational considerations influenced the composer in his decision to employ two opposing time signatures rather than one all-embracing meter.

From a purely technical standpoint the change in meter from the brass instruments' $\frac{3}{2}$ to the violins' $\frac{2}{2}$ understandably creates no basic rhythmic complications. Furthermore, within both meters the accompanying $\frac{6}{8}$ measures in the woodwinds merely constitute alternative notations for ♩-note value sextuplets in the measures of ♩-note denominators. In other words, the passage is not as difficult to interpret as the notation would lead one to expect.

Dual time signatures are frequently more than merely desirable in a

Ex. 5-24. Richard Wagner: *Götterdämmerung*, pp.1337–57

given rhythmic context; they may become mandatory in order to obviate the otherwise essential presence of a double set of numerals for certain complex unequal note groups. For example: in simple duple time ($\frac{2}{4}$ or $\frac{4}{4}$) a ♩-note triplet further subdivided into triplet ♪'s requires two sets of identifying numerical figures. This technical device can cause a measure to become notationally cluttered and to create unnecessary eyestrain for the performer. The most practical solution is to alter the meter of the irrational groups to compound time (sesquialtera). Thus only a single numeral is required over each ♪-note triplet group rather than a double set of figures with their corresponding horizontal brackets—certainly a welcome boon to the score reader.

Excellent proof of the incontestable pragmatism of such a solution is demonstrated in the prelude to Act I of Wagner's *Parsifal* (Ex. 5-25*a*). The composer's chordal background to his theme is notated in the compound meter of $\frac{6}{4}$ against $\frac{4}{4}$ to avoid having to use two sets of numerals. An alternative notation for Wagner's accompanimental pattern is given in part *b* of the example. While perfectly feasible—in modern terms, at least—such a solution would have been notationally extreme both for the period and for Wagner's inherent and habitual rhythmic conservatism.

The utilization of polymeters is often fully justified by virtue of a composer's combining two or more contrasting musical ideas that earlier in the work had been expressed separately with individual and nonagreeing time signatures. Clearly this premise largely explains Wagner's choice of dual signatures in the *Götterdämmerung* excerpt. As a somewhat later example of this premise, in the third act of Richard Strauss's *Der Rosenkavalier* a backstage orchestra continues to play a graceful waltz (the upper staff of Ex. 5-26) while the pit orchestra unfolds a broad theme in $\frac{4}{4}$, heard previously in Act I (lower staff). In this particular juxtaposition the three ♩ notes of the waltz meter are equal to one ♩ note of the main orchestral part; four measures of the former signature are thus required to equal one measure of the latter.[5]

Any other notational solution for this skillful blending of disparate musical ideas would have been awkward at best. An authentic waltz pulsation could hardly be convincingly imparted in $\frac{12}{8}$ (to accommodate four measures of triple meter in one of quadruple time), nor could the lyric flow of the $\frac{4}{4}$ theme be smoothly broken into four measures of duplets within an overall triple meter without sacrificing its inherent legato and total avoidance of inner accent. In addition to these technical considerations, a meter commonly shared by two contrasting musical ideas would, no less than in Mozart's case, effectively nullify the psychological aptness of Strauss's dramatic juxtaposition of emotional opposites.

Another clear illustration of the same kind of polymetric reasoning, though the work is symphonic rather than operatic, appears in Paul Hindemith's *Symphonia Serena*. In the final section of his third movement the composer combines sections one and two of the movement, each

---

5. An identical polymetrical situation occurs in Benjamin Britten's *War Requiem*, on pp.211–17 of the study score. Only the mood of the music, and not the rhythmic effect, differs from the Strauss citation.

Ex. 5-25. Richard Wagner: Prelude to *Parsifal*, p.2

a.

b.

etc.

bearing a different time signature. The opening material (in $\frac{4}{8}$, ♪ = 84), given to the first string orchestra group, is lyric in character (Ex. 5-27*a*); that of the succeeding Trio (in $\frac{2}{2}$, ♩ = 84), played by the second string group, is scherzo-like (*b*). Both sections are then literally combined (*c*), with no alterations of any kind until their respective final few measures.

Ex. 5-26. Richard Strauss: *Der Rosenkavalier*, p.358

If it were not for such an obvious juxtaposition of two highly contrasting ideas, each preserving its individual meter, tempo, accentuations, and character, one or the other of the dual time signatures used by

Ex. 5-27. Paul Hindemith: *Symphonia Serena*. © 1947 by Schott & Co. Ltd. Copyright renewed. Used with permission. All rights reserved.

a. p.61

b. p.64

c. p.68

Hindemith could—and probably would—have been altered so as to produce metrical conformity.

As a final example of this brand of polymetric justification: at the end of Act I of this writer's opera, *Villon,* a solo voice part in $\frac{6}{8}$ is set against the accompanying orchestra's $\frac{4}{4}$. The ♪ notes of each signature are mutually equal; hence the passage does not combine triplets with duplets but rather distributes the durationally uniform ♪'s with contrasting primary accents and measure lengths (Ex. 5-28*a*). As in each of the previously discussed quotations, an alternative and metrically co-equal notation was available; it seemed, however, to be both less precise and less psychologically correct for the dramatic situation at hand. Consequently the visually more complicated, yet far more realistic, notation was chosen.

Later in this scene there is a reprise of the solo voice part over the identical orchestral background; again the two elements of the musical fabric utilize the meters of $\frac{6}{8}$ and $\frac{4}{4}$. A third dramatic factor, however, is added to the scene by way of an extended timpani ostinato in $\frac{15}{8}$ (*b*). Although the ♪ notes of the $\frac{6}{8}$ and $\frac{4}{4}$ signatures again agree, they are in opposition to the ♪'s of the $\frac{15}{8}$ meter, these in effect being ♪-note triplets in $\frac{5}{4}$. The pulse in this ostinato is displaced by one ♪ note on each of four of the five primary beats of the $\frac{15}{8}$ measure, the pattern continuing inflexibly while the parts in $\frac{6}{8}$ and $\frac{4}{4}$ proceed independently.

Ex. 5-28. Gardner Read: *Villon*

a. p.133

b. p.154

Polymetric schemes that utilize variable or alternating changes of time signatures rather than remaining within two unvarying patterns are also to be found in many twentieth-century compositions. For example, in his early piano piece *Exultation*, Henry Cowell notated one measure each of $\frac{4}{4}$ and $\frac{5}{4}$ to fill the concurrent durational span of three $\frac{3}{4}$ measures. This sequence of changing signatures continues without alteration for the balance of the composition. Cowell's decision to use polymeters to express the rhythmic opposition between the two hands was far more logical than attempting to show the disagreement by means of phrasings or beamings over the barlines of a uniform $\frac{3}{4}$. In this case the separate autonomies of the melody (in the right hand) and the accompaniment (left hand) are not only preserved but are immeasurably strengthened by the psychological aptness of the dual signatures.

Another significant example of this technique—alternating meters versus an unchanging pattern—is found in the final section of Benjamin

Britten's *War Requiem*. Here, $\frac{2}{2}$ alternating with $\frac{3}{2}$ in the boys' choir is pitted against a flowing $\frac{2}{4}$ in solo tenor and baritone parts and orchestra (Ex. 5-29). The ♩ note of the treble voice part equals the ♩ note of the solo voice and orchestra lines; thus a $\frac{2}{2}$ and a $\frac{2}{4}$ measure have coequal durations, justified solely by the nature of the opposing musical materials.

Of particular interest is Britten's handling of the momentary cessation of the solo voice and orchestra parts. Rather than express this silence with the requisite rest symbols (four ♩-note values), the composer resorts to placing a fermata sign over the single ♩-note rest at the end of the measure. The following barline is then displaced so as to indicate that the resumption of the parts coincides with the second rather than the first half of the accompanying $\frac{2}{2}$ measure.

Ex. 5-29. Benjamin Britten: *War Requiem*, p.229

Boys'
choir
Orch.

Perhaps, parenthetically, it should be pointed out that composers do not always feel it essential to indicate polymetric signatures on the staff itself. Frequently notators show by means of miniaturized time signatures or other indicia above or below the staff the intended conflict between a prevailing pulsation and a superimposed rhythmic design. Shown in Ex. 5-30 are a few of the symbological methods currently favored by contemporary composers. They are, as it were, compromises between the explicit and the implicit.

In his ballet score *Facsimile*, Leonard Bernstein took great pains to designate the polymetric scheme of one instrumental voice, but kept his symbology on the staff in the customary manner (Ex. 5-31). By actually placing a second time signature in parentheses before the outset of the passage, in addition to including dotted barlines supplemented with phrasing slurs and staccato dots, the composer left no room for doubt as to the trimetric cross-accenting desired.

Although conceptually simple, a quite singular example of polymetric design occurs in Hindemith's *Concerto for Woodwinds, Harp and Orchestra* (last movement, beginning at letter K). It is uncommon because it juxtaposes alternating simple and compound time in the orchestral parts with a completely free and unmetered part for the solo harp.

Ex. 5-30

a. Arthur Bliss: *Quintet for Oboe and Strings*, p.54

b. Benjamin Britten: *Cantata Academica*, p.1

c. Aaron Copland: *First Symphony*, p.10

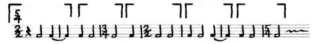

d. Aaron Copland: *Sextet for String Quartet, Clarinet and Piano*, p.13

e. Aaron Copland: *Short Symphony*, p.30

f. Aaron Copland: *Symphony for Organ and Orchestra*, p.30

g. Luigi Dallapiccola: *Due Pezzi per Orchestra*, p.15

h. Peter Maxwell Davies: *Shakespeare Music*, p.8

i. Roberto Gerhard: *Hymnody*, p.27

j. Leon Kirchner: *Trio for Violin, Cello and Piano*, p.21

k. Billy Jim Layton: *Divertimento*, p.2

l. Shinichi Matsushita: *Composizione da Camera per 8*, p.18

m. Igor Stravinsky: *Requiem Canticles*, p.1

As a composer for whom rhythmic regularity and strict metrical concurrence were the norm, Hindemith seldom indulged in such an
improvisatory approach to rhythmic contrast. Indeed, only one other
comparable instance comes to mind: the barless, *senza misura* part for
solo organ running concurrently with combined simple and compound
meters in the orchestra in Hindemith's 1962 organ concerto (refer to
p.75f of the study score).

We have already noted that rhythmic imitation within the ambience
of implicit polymeters is common to the music of Schoenberg and
Berg. The technique is, naturally, just as viable in the presence of
explicit polymeters. One of the most extended instances of actual
polymetric imitation occurs in Webern's second cantata, op. 31: the
entire sixth section of this work is canonic, even to the variable changes
of time signature for the individual voice parts (Ex. 5-32). Another
composer might have made the changes of meter agree in all the voices,
making liberal use of dotted notes and tie slurs to preserve the necessary
note values of the melodic canon. It is significant that Webern, a
composer for whom all aspects of polyphony were integral to his
compositional philosophy, chose to delineate in visually dramatic
terms the strict canonic progress of his musical statement.

Yet another instance of strict polymetric imitation is illustrated by
the *Sex Carmina Alcaei* (in the *Canon contrario motu*) of Dallapiccola.

Ex. 5-31. Leonard Bernstein: *Facsimile*, p.64

Ex. 5-32. Anton Webern: *II. Kantate*, op. 31, pp.48–52

Neither as complex nor as extended as the Webern canon just discussed, Dallapiccola's instrumental two-voice metrical imitation is still worthy of careful scrutiny (Ex. 5-33). A common factor in both quoted examples is that the note denominators are always, and of necessity, of equal value between the opposing signatures. In Webern's canon, ♩ note always equals ♩ note, while in the Dallapiccola excerpt, ♩. = ♩..

Ex. 5-33. Luigi Dallapiccola: *Sex Carmina Alcaei*, pp.18–20

This inventive Italian composer has demonstrated a peculiar fondness for certain devices of polyphonic imitation, notably the venerable technique of rhythmic augmentation. In his *Tartiniana Seconda*, for example, Dallapiccola employs dual triple meters so as to delineate more clearly the canonic imitation, in both inversion and augmentation, between his two melodic voices (Ex. 5-34). A parallel approach to metrical duality, imposed by strictly imitative contrapuntal elements, informs another extended passage in the composer's *Sex Carmina Alcaei* (Ex. 5-35).

Ex. 5-34. Luigi Dallapiccola: *Tartiniana Seconda*, p.42

Ex. 5-35. Luigi Dallapiccola: *Sex Carmina Alcaei*, p.27

When notators express two or more opposing plans, their choice of individual meter denominators can sometimes be both mentally and visually confusing. To cite several conspicuous examples: in Zoltán Kodály's *Psalmus Hungaricus* and in the fourth symphony of Charles Ives, there are combined passages of $\frac{6}{8}$ and $\frac{4}{4}$ whose respective barlines coincide (Ex. 5-36a). The two composers' basic premise is clear enough—to oppose simple and compound time—but their notational logic is faulty. The proper, more comprehensible, notation is to make the basic units of time agree, whether ♪ notes or ♩'s are chosen as denominators (*b* and *c*).

Ex. 5-36

a.   *b.*   *c.*

Also notationally puzzling are twin passages taken from Gunther Schuller's *Conversations for Jazz Quartet and String Quartet* and his *Journey into Jazz*, both of which juxtapose two conflicting versions of $\frac{4}{4}$, two measures of the one equalling one measure of the other (Ex. 5-37*a*). It would seem that either of the alternative notations (*b* and *c*) would be both more accurate in their relative note values and less confusing for the performer.

Ex. 5-37. Gunther Schuller: *Conversations for Jazz Quartet and String Quartet*, p.5; *Journey into Jazz*, p.24

a.   *b.*   *c.*

Several passages in Strauss's *Salomé* provide further notational puzzlements: at rehearsal number 283, for instance, the composer juxtaposes the meters of $\frac{5}{4}$ and $\frac{7}{4}$, with their respective barlines coinciding. Each meter is subdivided within the measure by means of a dotted barline, the $\frac{5}{4}$ as 2 + 3 and the $\frac{7}{4}$ as 3 + 4; the secondary barlines are likewise in agreement (Ex. 5-38*a*). Thus Strauss superimposes two different denominational versions of what is, in essence, simple duple over simple triple time. As the ♩ note of the $\frac{7}{4}$ meter equals the ♩ note of the preceding basic $\frac{3}{4}$ time signature, it is evident that Strauss's notational miscalculation lies in the choice of $\frac{5}{4}$ as the opposing meter; properly, this should also have been written as $\frac{7}{4}$, as shown in part *b* of the citation.

There are, however, two other options available in the notation of these measures, outlined in *c* and *d*, but each would have to be accompanied by an adjustment of tempo so that the total number of ♩ notes in either alternative version would exactly fill the time length of the original $\frac{7}{4}$ meter.

Ex. 5-38. Richard Strauss: *Salomé*, p.271

a.

b.

c.

d.

Another demonstration of questionable polymetric notation in *Salomé* occurs just before the beginning of the final scene. The problem here relates not only to the puzzling notation but also to the contradictory versions of these measures in the piano-vocal score (published by Fürstner) and in the full orchestral score (Boosey & Hawkes). A close examination of the two versions is instructive, to say the least (Ex. 5-39).

As will be seen, Strauss has juxtaposed a single $\frac{3}{2}$ measure over a continued pattern of ♩-note triplets in a basic $\frac{4}{4}$ meter in the vocal score (*a* of the example); in the full score this measure is notated as a $\frac{3}{4}$ over $\frac{3}{2}$, with the barlines in agreement—as they were in version *a*. Obviously, $\frac{3}{4}$ and $\frac{3}{2}$ cannot be made to coincide durationally; therefore one or the other of the dual time signatures should have been altered accordingly—obviously, the $\frac{3}{4}$ to $\frac{3}{2}$.

This particular measure is further complicated visually in the orchestral score by a rhythmic pattern in an explicit $\frac{6}{4}$ meter while at the same time other patterns are progressing in $\frac{4}{4}$. A fourfold notated polymetric scheme is thus in operation, although in reality only two opposing metrical schemes are perceived aurally—$\frac{3}{2}$ ($\frac{6}{4}$) and $\frac{4}{4}$, or the simultaneous combination of hemiola and sesquialtera. It would seem, consequently, that Strauss made his notation rather more complex than his rhythmical framework warranted.

Ex. 5-39. Ibid.

a. Fürstner edition, p.179

b. Boosey & Hawkes edition, p.297

Inkblot, an experimental symphonic band composition by Matthias Bamert, contains a curious passage that combines the signatures of $\frac{9}{8}$ and $\frac{2}{2}$ (Ex. 5-40). The ♪ notes of the two meters, however, are not co-equal; neither do the $\frac{9}{8}$ ♪'s signify triplets in $\frac{2}{2}$ ($\frac{4}{4}$). Instead, they actually represent ♩-note triplets, grouped here as 3 + 3 rather than 2 + 2 + 2. Or, alternatively, they designate triplet ♪'s, but in $\frac{2}{4}$ instead of $\frac{2}{2}$. In plain words, the composer's choice of notation is faulty; his polymeters should have been written either as $\frac{9}{8}$ over $\frac{2}{4}$ or as $\frac{9}{4}$ over $\frac{2}{2}$—the latter being the more logical of the two possibilities.

Ex. 5-40. Matthias Bamert: *Inkblot,* p.26

Far more rational is the combination of $\frac{3}{4}$ and $\frac{6}{8}$ in a passage taken from Robert Moevs's string quartet, even though the two meters here do not signify combined simple and compound time (hemiola). Instead, the $\frac{6}{8}$ signature represents two groups of triplet ♪ notes covering two

♩-note beats of the ¾ meter (Ex. 5-41). Barline concurrence thus takes place after three measures of the former and two measures of the latter signature.

Ex. 5-41. Robert Moevs: *String Quartet*, p.35

Polymeters, as previously noted in the discussion of irrational note groups, frequently serve as notational substitutes for complex irrational figures in one voice within a meter common to all parts. For example: on p.46 of his *Chants et Prismes*, Roman Haubenstock-Ramati has notated two instrumental lines in $\frac{5}{16}$ against $\frac{3}{8}$ in two other parts. Both meters serve as irregular manifestations of a basic $\frac{1}{4}$ operative in the balance of the orchestra—quintuplets and triplets, in other words, used concurrently with duplets. However, the other instruments proceeding in $\frac{1}{4}$ must frequently subdivide their measures into ♪-note sextuplets (or $\frac{6}{16}$) and quintuplets ($\frac{5}{16}$). The net result rhythmically is three polymeters operating concurrently: $\frac{1}{4}$ ($\frac{2}{8}$ or $\frac{4}{16}$), $\frac{3}{8}$ ($\frac{6}{16}$), and $\frac{5}{16}$—but with all barlines in consistent agreement. Complex as the aural result may be, it is surpassed by the visual intricacy confronting the score reader.

Psychological reasoning, which was nonetheless pragmatic in result, obviously led Hindemith to combine two different forms of compound triple time in his 1940 cello concerto. Both time signatures are $\frac{9}{8}$, but one extends to three measures within only one measure of the other, as shown on the central staves of Ex. 5-42. The ratio between the two meters is thus 3:1, or compound over simple triple time (sesquialtera). Hindemith might have expressed the top $\frac{9}{8}$ as $\frac{27}{16}$ (or 9/♪.) so as to represent ♪-note triplets within an overall $\frac{9}{8}$ measure (see the uppermost staff, in parentheses, of Ex. 5-42). Evidently the composer felt that such a choice would have been notationally awkward as well as destroying the related yet opposing character of the dual meters. An alternative and eminently practical solution would have been to accommodate the broader version of $\frac{9}{8}$ within the barlines of the more active part, as shown on the lowest staff in parentheses. This plan, however, would seem to bestow undue emphasis on the second and third ♩ notes in the part, obviously not what Hindemith intended.

Composers have none too rarely juxtaposed simultaneous time

Ex. 5-42. Paul Hindemith: *Concerto for Cello and Orchestra*, p.63

signatures that are far more complicated than necessary. In his fourth symphony, for instance (a veritable Pandora's box of rhythmic and metric complexities), Charles Ives notated several polymetric passages according to the values shown in Ex. 5-43*a* and 5-44*a*. A more realistic—certainly, a more practical—notation would read as indicated in part *b* of each example, or part *c* of the first.

Ex. 5-43. Charles Ives: *Symphony no. 4*, p.26

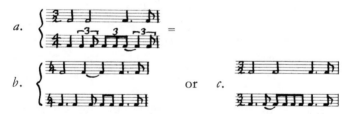

Ex. 5-44. Ibid., p.119

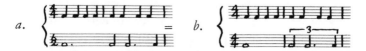

An equally faulty example appears in Dallapiccola's first *Tartiniana* for violin and orchestra (Ex. 5-45). A clearer, rhythmically justifiable alternative appears as the lowest line of the example. In none of these suggested alternate notations has the composers' premise of metrical opposition been violated, nor has the desired aural result been circumvented. But when given the choice between simplicity and convolution, any composer would do well to settle on the former—for the sake of the performer, if for no other reason.

On the other hand, the seemingly extreme coupling of $\frac{3}{4}$ and $\frac{4}{2}$ utilized by Ravel in his chamber trio can readily be justified by the

Ex. 5-45. Luigi Dallapiccola: *Tartiniana*, p.33

strikingly opposite rhythmic patterns, phrasings, and general character of the several parts (Ex. 5-46). The broad, legato nature of the piano part is effectively conveyed by the correspondingly broad meter of $\frac{4}{2}$, while the more animated and staccato qualities of the two string parts are aptly expressed by a time signature having a shorter note value as denominator and a smaller numerator. Thus the autonomy of each is preserved intact, the utilization of widely divergent polymetric signatures here being a stylistically and psychologically correct decision.

Ex. 5-46. Maurice Ravel: *Trio pour Violon, Violoncelle et Piano*, p.15

Not all explicit polymeters are actually polymetric. In the Dallapiccola work of Ex. 5-45, for instance, a passage on p.50 of the study score combines a pattern of two measures of $\frac{2}{4}$ with one of $\frac{2}{2}$. As the stresses and internal note groupings within both meters are so uniform and in such normal agreement one with the other, there seems little justification in this instance for dual time signatures. Both parts could—and should—have been accommodated by a single meter; whether $\frac{2}{4}$ or $\frac{2}{2}$, no damage to the composer's basic idea would result.

There are times, of course, when visually complex schemata of simultaneous time signatures may be completely justified in that they are the only way the composer can accurately express the conflicting framework of rhythm. As a specific instance: at one point in his oboe and string quintet, Arthur Bliss combines the signatures of $\frac{6}{8}$ and $\frac{7}{8}$, but the ♪ notes are not of coequal duration (Ex. 5-47a). Close inspection of this passage reveals that the two rhythmic patterns are at the ratio of 6:4; that is to say, they represent the simultaneous use of simple and compound time, or $\frac{6}{8}$ over $\frac{4}{8}$ ($\frac{2}{4}$). Because, however, the nominal $\frac{4}{8}$ meter embraces a constantly recurring, seven-note ostinato figure—which is grouped in the form 3 + 2 + 2—it is entirely logical that the composer has notated this line as a series of $\frac{7}{8}$ measures. Beaming the seven-note groups over the barlines of $\frac{4}{8}$ is certainly a notational possibility (*b*), but it is one less unequivocal. Furthermore, the consistent accentual design would thereby fall on different portions of the $\frac{4}{8}$ measures—not at all what the composer intended.

Ex. 5-47. Arthur Bliss: *Quintet for Oboe and Strings*, p.48

a.

b.

A related polymetrical situation occurs in Henri Pierné's violin sonata—related in that the visually complicated polymeters actually represent the clearest manner of showing the contrasting rhythms desired by the composer (Ex. 5-48*a*). In essence, the $\frac{6}{8}$ violin part constitutes triplets in duple time, while the piano part in $\frac{10}{16}$ represents quintuplets in duple time. It should be obvious that notating both parts with a commonly shared time signature would create unnecessary reading problems by cluttering the measures with gratuitous numerals and ancillary brackets in each part (*b*).

Ex. 5-48. Henri Gabriel Pierné: *Sonate pour Violon et Piano*, p.1

a.   *b.*

An equally intricate-appearing, yet inherently simple, polymetric juxtaposition occurs in Bartók's second string quartet (Ex. 5-49). As can be seen, the $^{3+4}_{8}$ meter overlaps the barlines of the $\frac{6}{8}$ signature by an arithmetical process, adding one more ♪ note each time the pattern extends beyond the $\frac{6}{8}$ barlines. This process is the direct reversal of that employed by Messiaen in his previously cited organ work, *Le Verbe* (Ex. 5-6), where the composer subtracted one unit of his meter denominator on each repetition of the pattern.

Ex. 5-49. Béla Bartók: *String Quartet no. 2*, p.7

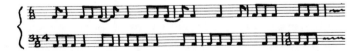

The meters of $\frac{4}{4}$ and $\frac{7}{8}$, joined synchronistically, are required by Lejaren Hiller in his *String Quartet no. 5* (p.24), as are $\frac{5}{8}$ against $\frac{7}{8}$ on later pages. In both passages the ♪ notes are coequal. Seven measures of the $\frac{4}{4}$ ($\frac{8}{8}$) meter equal eight measures of the $\frac{7}{8}$, at which point all parts share a common barline. In the second instance it takes seven measures of $\frac{5}{8}$ and five measures of $\frac{7}{8}$ to bring the opposing voices to barline coincidence.

At the very outset of Charles Ives's problematic fourth symphony the composer combines two time signatures with coequal denominators ($\frac{6}{4}$ and $\frac{3}{4}$), but quite effectively destroys the validity of the $\frac{6}{4}$ meter by dividing the entire measure into an irrational note group. Furthermore, at the same time, the $\frac{3}{4}$ meter is superimposed upon $\frac{6}{8}$ (hemiola) and, in another orchestral part, is divided into measure quintuplets (Ex. 5-50). Thus, four metrical patterns are in operation throughout the passage.

The notational problem here truly defies an alternative solution; combining two $\frac{3}{4}$ measures into one $\frac{6}{4}$ measure does not simplify the issue, nor would altering the $\frac{6}{4}$ meter to $\frac{5}{2}$ in order to obviate the repeated quintuplet numerals. Many of the irrational note groups disguised as polymeters in the fourth symphony and in certain other Ives compositions can be simplified in their notation, but this instance does not appear to be one of them.

Ex. 5-50. Charles Ives: *Symphony no. 4*, p.2

The question is perhaps moot whether or not the widely prevalent practice of notating simultaneous simple and compound time (sesquialtera) with dual time signatures ought to be regarded as an authentically polymetrical technique. Such occurrences may nearly always be explained on the grounds of notational expediency. The utilization of two different time signatures is only validated by the extent to which triplets, let us say, are pitted against duplets, or vice versa. In other words, a lengthy passage of threes against twos or fours is more easily accommodated by the concurrent use of compound and simple time, expressed with corresponding meters and obviating the incessant and notationally awkward inclusion of irrational-figure numerals and brackets.

This reasoning evidently dictated the use of three different meter signatures, appearing concurrently, in the first movement of Ralph Vaughan Williams's sixth symphony. In combination with simple time, here expressed by the signature of $\frac{2}{2}$, the composer notates two different versions of compound time; the technique of hemiola is thus an important element in the cross-rhythmic web (Ex. 5-51).

Ex. 5-51. Ralph Vaughan Williams: *Symphony no. 6*, p.34

Speaking ostensibly as a theorist rather than as a composer, Hindemith once stated: "The use of ♩ and ♩. together as equivalent representatives of a single value is not possible without causing the greatest confusion."[6] This observation now seems excessively conservative and cautious, Hindemith's practical experience notwithstanding, for composers have been combining simple and compound time, expressed with dual time signatures, since at least the Classical period (Ex. 5-23, for instance; and refer also to Mozart's *Oboe Quartet*, K. 370, the third movement). Indeed, Hindemith himself has often combined two time signatures representing compound and simple time, a fact that considerably weakens his contention.

One prominent example is to be found in the composer's wind septet, fifth movement, where the signature of 4/♩. , representing $\frac{12}{8}$, is

6. *Elementary Training for Musicians* (New York: Associated Music Publishers, Inc., 1949), p.115.

pitted against $\frac{2}{2}$. The latter signature is entrusted solely to the trumpet part, which never deviates from simple time through the course of the movement. The remaining instruments, in metrical parallel, never venture outside of compound time. Obviously, then, the only practical solution in the matter of meter was that chosen by the composer.

A further instance of Hindemith's self-contradicting utilization of combined simple and compound time signatures occurs in his overture to the opera *Neues vom Tage*, where $\frac{9}{8}$ and $\frac{3}{4}$ operate simultaneously for many pages (beginning on p.44). And in the movement for wind instruments alone of the *Symphonia Serena* (p.49) Hindemith couples $2/\mathrm{d}$. (or $\frac{6}{4}$) and $\frac{2}{2}$ for the duration of some forty-six measures—hardly a casual allusion to the sesquialtera technique or an apologetic use of concurrent meters with differing denominator values.

The same reasoning that led Vaughan Williams to combine two versions of compound with one of simple time (Ex. 5-51) dictated several polymetric passages in the *Shakespeare Music* of Peter Maxwell Davies. One sequence combines $\frac{9}{4}$ and $\frac{18}{8}$ with $\frac{3}{2}$, the first two signatures standing for triplets and sextuplets in the basic $\frac{3}{2}$ meter. Immediately following, the composer pairs $\frac{15}{8}$ and $\frac{6}{4} + \frac{3}{8}$ with $\frac{5}{4}$, again representing the combination of two versions of compound time with simple time. On the sequent page Davies combines $\frac{6}{4}$ and $\frac{12}{8}$ with $\frac{4}{4}$ ($\frac{2}{2}$) but further enriches the texture by the addition of $\frac{14}{8}$, or two septuple grouplets in the underlying meter of $\frac{2}{2}$. An examination of pp.31–35 of the study score will clarify the composer's contextual handling of his polymeters.

A more homogeneous juxtaposition of compound and simple time, expressed by two different meter signatures, is located in the sixth symphony of Karl Amadeus Hartmann. Here, $\frac{3}{4}$ and $\frac{2}{4}$ are combined, with their barlines in agreement, but with the indication that the $\frac{3}{4}$ should be grouped in four-measure segments. Essentially, this creates the metrical feeling of $\frac{12}{4}$ against $\frac{8}{4}$—a rather disguised version of sesquialtera (Ex. 5-52).

On p.54 of Elliott Carter's *Sonata for Flute, Oboe, Cello and Harpsichord*, one finds the metric juxtaposition of $\frac{6}{8}$ and $4/\mathrm{J}$·, the latter signature being the translation of a full measure quadruplet in $\frac{3}{4}$. In his third string quartet Carter combines $\frac{3}{2}$, $\frac{12}{8}$, and $\frac{24}{16}$ (on p.27), the latter two meters representing two different versions of compound grouping. Incidentally, in a somewhat later section of the quartet Carter utilizes a measure of exceptional metrical length: $\frac{27}{32}$ over $\frac{3}{4} + \frac{3}{32}$ (p.75). Measures of such durational span are difficult for performers to negotiate, as normal points of stress become tenuous.

Two versions each of simple and compound time operate on the final page of George Crumb's *Black Angels* (Ex. 5-53). To a quadri-partite texture consisting of $\frac{3}{2}$ and $\frac{3}{4}$, $\frac{12}{8}$ and $\frac{6}{4}$, the composer adds yet another compound meter, $\frac{9}{8}$, but begins its course in mid-measure of the other parts so that an overlapping of barlines momentarily results. The unifying factor in this mélange of meters is the ♩ note at M.M. 60, which has the same durational value in all the signatures, though accents and phrasings predictably differ in each.

Ex. 5-52. Karl Amadeus Hartmann: *6. Symphonie*, p.116

Ex. 5-53. George Crumb: *Black Angels*, p.9

Although authentic sesquialtera is not involved in the next score quotation, the composer Boguslaw Schäffer manifestly chose to combine simple duple and compound triple time to obviate his writing a protracted series of irrational note groups in the basic meter of $\frac{3}{8}$ (Ex. 5-54). Against this triple pulse Schäffer pits a number of measures in $\frac{2}{4}$, each containing four ♪ notes. This particular juxtaposition of meters is quite elementary, of course, and many composers faced with notating the same kind of simple rhythmic opposition would no doubt choose to remain in a single meter. Because the notational problem in this case is a minor one and can be solved satisfactorily either way, the choice of format is entirely subjective.

A somewhat more involved conjoining of meters occurs on page

Ex. 5-54. Boguslaw Schäffer: *Quattro movimenti per pianoforte e orchestra*, p.103

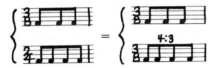

two of *Metastaseis* by Iannis Xenakis; the composer's avoidance here of having to notate conflicting and constantly recurring note groups in several different parts is the rationale for his polymetric scheme. Xenakis's intent is clearly evident in the designation placed over the initial measure: $\frac{4}{16} = \frac{3}{8} = \frac{5}{16} = \downarrow = 60$ M.M.

The *Introduzione–Sequenze–Coda* of the Swedish composer Bengt Hambraeus contains one fairly extended section that combines $\frac{5}{4}$, $\frac{4}{4}$, and $\frac{3}{4}$, but with all barlines in agreement (pp.39–41 of the score). Inasmuch as $\frac{4}{4}$ is the prevailing meter in the majority of instruments, the $\frac{5}{4}$ and $\frac{3}{4}$ signatures are alternative notations for measure quintuplets and triplets. Later in the work the composer indicates the polymetric patterns shown in Ex. 5-55a. A possible substitute notation is suggested at *b*, though the distinction is perhaps only academic.

Ex. 5-55. Bengt Hambraeus: *Introduzione–Sequenze–Coda*, p.45

a.   *b.*

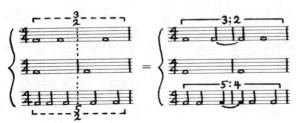

Appropriately subtitled *Scherzo polymetrico*, the second movement of Edmund Rubbra's *String Quartet no. 2* contains a lengthy passage of $\frac{21}{8}$ in two of the instruments against $\frac{12}{8}$ and $\frac{9}{8}$ measures in the remaining instruments. The ♪ notes in all the signatures are of equal duration. All four string parts might easily have been accommodated by a single time signature; this solution, however, would have weakened an essential ingredient in the composer's expression—namely, the individual melodic phrasings and the disparate character of the four voices.

In the finale of his *Spring Symphony* (p.119 of the study score), Benjamin Britten combines a strongly accented $\frac{2}{4}$ with a lilting, almost waltzlike $\frac{3}{4}$, their respective barlines in concurrence. The dual meters here are largely determined by the choral text of the boys' choir, the duple meter of "Soomer is icoomen in" being superimposed on a continuing mixed chorus texture of canonically imitated "*ah's*" in triple time. Both the nature of the musical materials and the inherent stresses of the chosen text, therefore, determined the psychological aptness of Britten's metrical duality in this lengthy section.

To combine simple and compound time signatures whose respective total number of beats within the measure do not produce barline coincidence is more authentically to create a polymetrical texture. The third movement of Hindemith's early *Kammermusik nr. 2* offers a prime example of this rhythmic condition (Ex. 5-56). Here the $\frac{3}{8}$ measures are not triplets within the $\frac{4}{4}$ meter of the piano part, but represent a beat and a half of that signature.

Ex. 5-56. Paul Hindemith: *Kammermusik nr. 2*, p.54. © 1924 by B. Schott's Söhne. Copyright renewed. Used with permission. All rights reserved.

Triple and duple meters in simple time whose denominators are of equal duration but whose barlines are not in concurrence appear in many twentieth-century works. One such example, familiar to analysts of Bartók's music, occurs in the third string quartet (Ex. 5-57). Super-imposed triple and duple ♩-note denominator values may be seen in operation in Hindemith's symphony *Mathis der Maler* (Ex. 5-58), where the composer overlays the Gregorian "Es sungen drei Engel" on his continuing second theme of the first movement.

Ex. 5-57. Béla Bartók: *String Quartet no. 3*, p.23

Ex. 5-58. Paul Hindemith: *Mathis der Maler*, p.20

A parallel example of polymetrical texture is to be found on the penultimate page of Ives's first string quartet: Violin I and Viola are in ¾ while Violin II and Cello progress in ⁴⁄₄, all ♩ notes of coequal value. And in the second movement (on p.12) of the second quartet, Violins I and II in ⁴⁄₄–¾ are paired with Viola and Cello in ⅜. Here the ♪ note of each signature is of the same duration. To this relatively simple juxtaposition of different meters Ives adds rhythmic complications by cross-accenting in one of the violin parts so that the measure stresses of the two ⁴⁄₄–¾ meters are not uniform. Immediately thereafter the composer reverses his time signature duality so that the violins operate in ⅜ and the lower string instruments in ⁴⁄₄, this time with a fair degree of accentual uniformity.

Several pages of Ives's *A Set of Pieces* are enlivened by a more radical juxtaposition of opposing time signatures, particularly in the second movement, illustrated in Ex. 5-59. While the timpani perseveres in a syncopated but unchanging ²⁄₄, the balance of the orchestra incessantly changes meter, creating a fascinating clash of basic pulsation between the two instrumental protagonists.

Ex. 5-59. Charles Ives: *In the Inn*, from *A Set of Pieces*, p.10

As previously noted, ostinati in triple time or in a triple pattern within duple or irregular meters are a hallmark of Stravinsky's rhythmic style—even in a work as late in his oeuvre as *Agon*. During the "Bransle Gay" section of Part II (Ex. 5-60) castanets maintain a delicate and explicit $\frac{3}{8}$ design through numerous meter changes in the other instrumental parts. This is a rhythmic device that goes all the way back to Stravinsky's early *Chant du Rossignol* (see Ex. 5-8), and that appears in many of his later scores.

Ex. 5-60. Igor Stravinsky: *Agon*, p.54

One of the most astonishing examples of a polymetric texture—from the visual standpoint, at the very least—ornaments the pages of Ives's amusing compositional spoof, *In Re Con Moto Et Al*. Against an undeviating $\frac{4}{4}$ meter in the solo piano part, the accompanying string quartet indulges in the following sequence of wildly irregular time-signature changes: $\frac{11}{4}$–$\frac{7}{8}$–$\frac{5}{4}$–$\frac{3}{4}$–$\frac{2}{4}$–$\frac{3}{4}$–$\frac{5}{4}$ (the first instance of barline concurrence with the piano part)–$\frac{11}{4}$–$\frac{33}{16}$–$\frac{21}{16}$–$\frac{15}{16}$–$\frac{9}{16}$–$\frac{6}{16}$ (the second mutual barline agreement)–$\frac{2}{8}$–$\frac{3}{8}$–$\frac{5}{8}$–$\frac{7}{8}$–$\frac{11}{8}$–$\frac{4}{4}$ (at which point the piano and strings are finally in consistent metrical agreement!).

If there is an arithmetical plan behind these changes, it eludes discovery by this analyst. As one might expect, no single instrumental voice in this polyrhythmical mélange, stretching over some six pages of score, is devoid of syncopation, cross-accenting, irrational figures, or any other irregular accentual devices.

The polymetric complexities of Ives are nearly equalled by those present in Elliott Carter's *String Quartet no. 1*. In addition to the relatively conservative juxtapositions of simple and compound time—$\frac{6}{4}$

over $\frac{2}{2}$, $\frac{5}{4}$ over $\frac{15}{8}$, $\frac{9}{8}$ over $\frac{3}{4}$, and $\frac{9}{16}$ over $\frac{3}{8}$—Carter pairs together such signatures as $\frac{2}{2}$ and $\frac{10}{8}$, $\frac{3}{2}$ and $\frac{15}{8}$, $\frac{6}{8}$ and $\frac{10}{16}$, $\frac{3}{2}$ and $\frac{21}{8}$, $\frac{20}{16}$ and $\frac{9}{8}$, and $\frac{18}{16}$ and $\frac{9}{8}$. In each instance all barlines are in congruity.

A particularly salient example of meter opposition occurs in the opening movement of the Carter quartet (Ex. 5-61). One obvious question comes immediately to mind on scanning this passage: why did Carter not go one step further in his acceptance of metrical duality and notate his Violin I part in $\frac{5}{4}$, with $\jmath$. $\jmath$ equalling the $\jmath$. of the other voices? The visually cluttered quintuplet numerals and brackets offend the eye, which, at best, has sufficient complications with which to cope. That Carter is essentially concerned with clarifying perplexing notational questions is proven by his alternative and simplified rhythmic version for Violin II. A similar gesture toward the score-reader (and performer) would have been appreciated.

Ex. 5-61. Elliott Carter: *String Quartet no. 1*, p.31. © 1951 by Associated Music Publishers, Inc. Used by permission.

Henry Cowell's brief *Quartet Euphometric* (apt title!) is a unique example of simultaneous meters. In addition to using conventional juxtapositions of meter, such as $\frac{5}{4} + \frac{3}{4} + \frac{2}{4}$ ($\downarrow = \downarrow$), the work exhibits the unusual combinations of $\frac{4}{4} + \frac{4}{6} + \frac{5}{6}$ and of $\frac{8}{6} + \frac{5}{6} + \frac{3}{4} + \frac{9}{16}$. Sixth notes used as denominator values derive, of course, from Cowell's early experiments with fractional rhythms and meters, discussed in an earlier chapter (see p.101). Note values within the quartet measures based on sixth-note denominators range from the $\frac{1}{24}$ note to the $\frac{2}{3}$ note (see Ex. 4-19*b*).

The work bears testimony to the young composer's inquiring mind and compositional boldness (he was nineteen when he composed the quartet). That Cowell did not continue to use his theoretical discoveries, such as fractional polymeters, in subsequent works was perhaps the result of his lifelong "urge toward further discovery," as one writer put it. In addition, the inherent complexities of both the concepts and their notations were no doubt inhibiting factors, discouraging Cowell from systematic continuance of his rhythmic ideas.

The most extreme applications of the principle of polymetric opposition occur either when the meters involved contain widely differing denominator values or when different tempi apply to the parts within each meter. Nearly every page of Mauricio Kagel's early string sextet illustrates the first metrical premise, the quotation in Ex. 5-62 being prototypical. Four different denominational note values are in operation here: $\downarrow$, $\downarrow$, $\downarrow$, and $\downarrow$. Even though these four time units and their component subdivisions are coequal within each metrical framework, shifts of accent and the addition of various irrational figures effectively cancel out any impression of orderly coincidence of pulsation.

As an outstanding exemplar of the second polymetric premise—simultaneous different tempi combined with opposing time signatures—we cite Lejaren Hiller's fifth string quartet, *Variation Twelve* (Ex. 5-63). Each instrument observes not only its own individual meter signature but also its own singular tempo indication. According to the composer's plan, three measures of a fairly rapid $\frac{4}{4}$, five measures of a scherzando $\frac{5}{8}$, and three measures of a moderate $\frac{3}{4}$ are roughly coequal with one measure of a slow $\frac{11}{8}$. It is evident that strict simultaneity of beat does not result—unless by coincidence—until the first mutually shared barline is reached. The composer does not attempt to line up the beats between the four parts in any scientific manner; only the barlines of the $\frac{4}{4}$ and $\frac{3}{4}$ parts are in union, by virtue of their respective, mathematically related metronomic indications.

Ex. 5-62. Mauricio Kagel: *Sexteto de cuerdas*, p.13. © 1962 by Universal Edition, Ltd. Used by permission of Universal Edition.

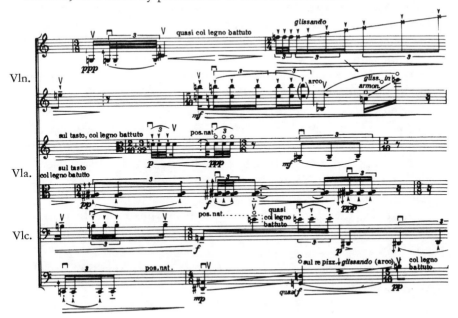

Another noteworthy instance of combined polymetricality and simultaneous tempi occurs in Hans Werner Henze's virtuosic *Compases para preguntas ensimismadas* for solo viola and orchestra. Not as rhythmically complex as the Hiller excerpt but far more protracted in duration, the passage combines a basic $\frac{3}{4}$ meter in the solo part and certain orchestral instruments with $\frac{4}{4}$ in the harp and harpsichord parts. (See pp.71–80 of the study score.) For those instruments in $\frac{3}{4}$ the tempo is ♩ = 66; for those in $\frac{4}{4}$ it is ♩ = 80. Not only do the respective barlines of the two meters generally disagree, but their sporadic concurrence is a result more of notational expediency than of arithmetical calculation.

Ex. 5-63. Lejaren Hiller: *String Quartet no. 5*, p.47

There are several polymetric passages in *Fluxus* of Girolamo Arrigo based on the same premise; one of these is illustrated in Ex. 5-64. Not only do the differing meters begin at nonconcurring moments but each part contains numerous irrational rhythmic groupings within its individual pattern of pulsations. In several other similarly conceived sections within this work, not cited here, the separate and disjunct metrical plans include double irrational figures within one or the other of the superimposed and overlapping polymeters—surely a case of carrying coals to Newcastle! Inasmuch as the validity of any unequal rhythmic subdivisions, regardless of the operative meter, depends upon an unmistakable relationship to the normal counting units in force, few performers will be able to produce accurately and confidently such irrational figures when no conductor's beat is present to establish the norm from which the irregular rhythms depart.

Two final examples of polymetric and tempo duality are drawn from *Winds* by Marius Constant and *Inside Outside* of Enrique Raxach. The

Ex. 5-64. Girolamo Arrigo: *Fluxus*, p.25. © 1963 by Aldo Bruzzichelli. Used by permission.

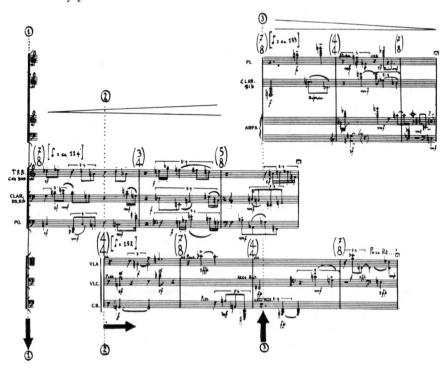

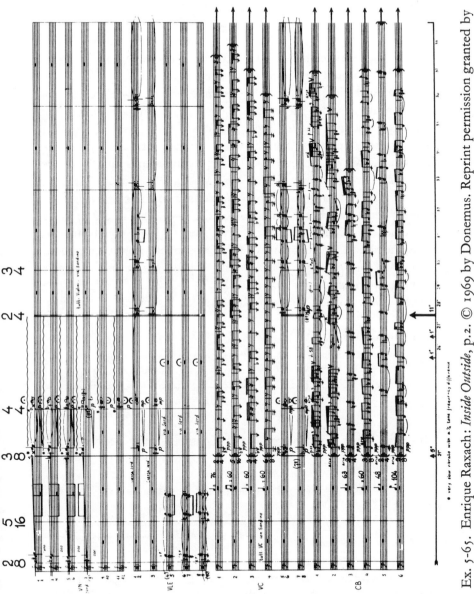

Ex. 5-65. Enrique Raxach: *Inside Outside*, p.2. © 1969 by Donemus. Reprint permission granted by C. F. Peters Corporation, New York; sole selling agents for the Western Hemisphere.

aural impression gained from Raxach's metrical free-for-all (Ex. 5-65) defies rational description and evaluation. With nine different meters operating synchronistically and governed by as many tempo ratios, it should be evident that the total effect will be no different from that produced by free improvisational procedures within an overall time span. In fact, this technique forms the basis for page 29 of Raxach's score, which should be compared with page 2.

Close inspection of the passage from *Winds* (Ex. 5-66) reveals that the seven measures of $\frac{2}{4}$ at ♩ note = 69 and the nine measures of $\frac{3}{4}$ at ♩ note = 126 ought not to agree precisely in time span, as they do in the composer's notation; in addition, the single $\frac{4}{4}$ measure, ♩ note at 63, should take only 3.84 seconds, yet is made to agree in timing with three measures of the part in $\frac{3}{4}$, which require a duration of 4.32 seconds. Furthermore, the barlines of the $\frac{2}{4}$ voice ought to coincide exactly with those of the $\frac{6}{8}$ part but do not do so; the two meters here represent combined simple and compound time, hence are of equal duration.

Mathematical precision may well be inimical to the composer's concept in this passage, which would explain his casual, if not inaccurate, approach to its notation. If this be so, a completely nonmetrical framework might better have served his intent.

Ex. 5-66. Marius Constant: *Winds*, p.18

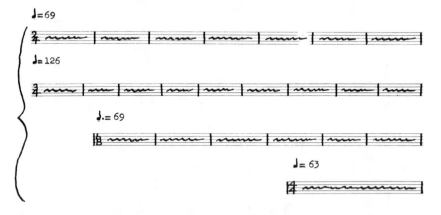

Innumerable additional archetypes of polymetrical occurrence, both inherently simple and calculatedly complex in nature, can easily be located in the music of today's serious composers. An analysis of various simultaneous time signatures in works not discussed on these pages—especially those operative in the complete works of Charles

Ives—would be highly instrumental in one's gaining further insights into the fundamental psychology of polymetric techniques. A significant case might be established that certain aleatoric and nonmetrical expressions of current avant-gardists are in reality only differently notated instances of hypercomplex polyrhythmic designs and so are not, as might be reasonably assumed, durational schemata purposely antimetrical in intent.

To turn this contention around: it could also be quite persuasively reasoned that many polymetric passages in contemporary scores—especially those occurring in Ives's fourth symphony, to cite a particularly trenchant specimen of metrical multiplicity—produce the aural equivalent of an unmetered and rhythmically ambivalent texture, such as might be found in any recent score by Berio, Ligeti, or Penderecki, among others. The choice, then, between metrical polarity and the total avoidance of meter becomes a subjective one; objectively, the boundary lines are too tenuous and the aural distinctions too inconclusive in many instances to determine the superiority of one technique over the other.

Nonetheless, in the final analysis, both as psychological reasoning and as technical methodology, the presence of polymeters, implicit and explicit alike, in the music of our time continues to have indisputable relevancy and to produce rhythmic autonomy and expressive conviction of singular vitality.

Afterword

The moment seems appropriate to pose a few questions concerning rhythmic practice in the music of our time. Are, for instance, the more abstruse complexities discussed and amply illustrated on the foregoing pages absolutely indispensable to contemporary musical expression? Can, or should, any of the more rarefied techniques of rhythmic delineation be modified, even radically simplified, and if so, can they still retain their validity as advanced rhythmic conceptualities? Should certain rhythmic practices favored by experimental-minded composers —fractional measure beats, let us say—be abandoned in preference to less esoteric concepts of fundamental beat subdivision? Should practicality and lucidity be the prime criteria for rhythmic ideas and their notations?

The answers to these and other related questions, one may be sure, will range from insistence on the doctrinaire application of every known mathematical theorem pertinent to musical rhythm and meter to rather ambivalent pleading for at least token acceptance of rhythmic irreducibility. Some composers and theorists, of course, will scorn the questions themselves as essentially meaningless. It seems likely that Milton Babbitt, Pierre Boulez, Karlheinz Stockhausen, and Charles Wuorinen, *inter alia*, would feel that to question even momentarily the more extreme rhythmic concepts and related techniques in contemporary music is not merely treasonous but is irrelevant. Other composers, including those whose personal convictions as to the absolute necessity for metrical and multirhythmical abstraction are just as strong, may privately acknowledge the desirability of pragmatic modifications in the compositional applications of advanced rhythmic design and structure.

Not a few composers and theory experts will remain relatively indifferent to the matter, caring little one way or another as to what consensus is established in the area of permutational meter and rhythm. Still others will continue to find satisfaction in their straightforward, "no-nonsense" attitude toward the rhythmic factor in their music, whether this is engendered by creative conservatism or is the result of excessive concern for the perceptual capabilities of their performers.

We find ourselves, therefore, largely where we were before the questions were posed. As musicians of the late twentieth century we are the inheritors of a vast corpus of music that reveals striking polarities of rhythmic concept, perception, and practice. The spectrum extends from the calculated naïvetés of Carl Orff to the inscrutabilities of Pierre Boulez; it embraces the tradition-oriented practices of Bartók, Britten, Hindemith, Prokofiev, Stravinsky, and Webern as well as the experiments of the advocates of proportionate notation—Berio, Earle Brown, George Crumb, Ligeti, Penderecki, and countless others. Who is to say which rhythmic concept, which technique, is best? Who is to say there is "a best"? The viability of any technique, rhythmic or otherwise, resides in the conviction and effectiveness with which it is employed by the composer. The merits of fractional meters, for example, can be neither proved nor disproved by objective criteria alone; the technique is valid when it produces a creative immutability in the composer's music; it is not valid when it is used to be "in fashion" or to assume compositional insights that are totally lacking in the creator's intellectual attributes.

Yet, when all the arguments and counterproposals have been made, and when every composer has made a subjective choice as to parametral philosophy and methodology, certain nagging reservations do remain. They basically have to do with the inevitable conflict between theory and practice, between what is possible (sometimes, barely so) on paper and what is achievable in human performance. Were the results of all rhythmic experimentation to be realized by a digital computer for performance on sound tape, there would then be no need for any questioning. The answers would be satisfactorily provided by the loudspeakers functioning for the benefit of the listener. But as all contemporary composition is not designed for electronic interpretation (if that is the correct term), the questions must still be framed and the answers still anticipated.

It is perfectly legitimate to inquire at this point: can the rhythmic and metric autonomies of the compositions cited in this study be fully comprehended and accurately interpreted by the performer? Can they be as clearly perceived by the listener? Or does it really matter, one way or another? Is the proposition moot, or can *Augenmusik* be convincingly justified in the context of experimental expression?

The eventual answers to all these queries may possibly suggest to the composer that the hypercomplex rhythms that are virtually impossible to notate simply and lucidly may be best achieved by discarding all pretense at mathematical accuracy and by allowing controlled freedom to produce the intricacies desired. Optical, or "time," notation can thus serve the rhythmic interests of the composer today far more effectively than the most ingenious devisings on paper could ever hope to accomplish. Far from begging the question of modern rhythmic complexity, this approach may well be the way to secure its ultimate solution.

Appendixes

Appendix A *Nonstandard Time Signatures*

1. WHOLE-NOTE DENOMINATORS.

a. $\frac{1}{1}$
  H. Birtwistle: 2*
  E. Blackwood: 1
  P. M. Davies: 3
  P. Boulez: 4
  K. Stockhausen: 15

b. $\frac{2}{1}$
  P. Boulez: 4
  P. M. Davies: 2
  A. Schoenberg: 1
  R. Sessions: 4

c. $\frac{3}{1}$
  P. M. Davies: 2
  C. Ives: 16
  E. London
  C. Orff: 1
  A. Prevost
  R. Sessions: 4
  K. Stockhausen: 15, 17
  O. Toni

d. $\frac{4}{1}$
  P. Boulez: 4
  P. M. Davies: 2
  C. Orff: 1
  O. Toni

e. $\frac{5}{1}$
  P. Boulez: 4
  D. Del Tredici: 2

f. $\frac{6}{1}, \frac{7}{1}$
  No examples located

g. $\frac{8}{1}$
  P. Boulez: 4
  C. Orff: 1

h. $\frac{9}{1}-$
  No examples located

2. HALF-NOTE DENOMINATORS.

a. $\frac{1}{2}-\frac{6}{2}$
  Examples too numerous to cite

b. $\frac{7}{2}$
  H. Cowell: 5
  R. Gerhard: 1
  C. Ives: 16
  C. Orff: 1
  A. Webern: 1

* Refer to Index of Composers and Works for coded numbers. Names not followed by a number indicate single entries in the Index.

c. $\frac{8}{2}$
    C. Ives: 16
    C. Orff: 1

d. $\frac{9}{2}$
    C. Ives: 8

e. $\frac{10}{2}, \frac{11}{2}$
    No examples located

f. $\frac{12}{2}$
    L. Bernstein: 2
    R. Harris: 1

g. $\frac{13}{2}-$
    No examples located

3. QUARTER-NOTE DENOMINATORS.

a. $\frac{1}{4}-\frac{12}{4}$
    Examples too numerous to cite

b. $\frac{13}{4}$
    J. Gilboa
    B. Nilsson: 2
    I. Stravinsky: 14

c. $\frac{14}{4}$
    J. Gilboa
    C. Wuorinen: 9

d. $\frac{15}{4}$
    J. Gilboa
    A. Hovhaness: 1
    B. Nilsson: 2
    G. Schuller: 2

e. $\frac{16}{4}$
    J. Gilboa
    C. Wuorinen: 9

f. $\frac{17}{4}$
    W. Albright: 2
    J. Gilboa

g. $\frac{18}{4}, \frac{19}{4}$
    J. Gilboa

h. $\frac{20}{4}$
    No examples located

i. $\frac{21}{4}$
    J. Gilboa
    A. Hovhaness: 1
    T. Mayuzumi: 1
    C. Wuorinen: 9

j. $\frac{22}{4}, \frac{23}{4}$
    No examples located

k. $\frac{24}{4}$
    C. Orff: 1
    C. Wuorinen: 6

l. $\frac{25}{4}-$
    C. Wuorinen: 6

4. EIGHTH-NOTE DENOMINATORS.

a. $\frac{1}{8}-\frac{12}{8}$
    Examples too numerous to cite

b. $\frac{13}{8}$
    B. Bartók: 2
    W. Heider: 2
    L. Janáček: 2
    L. Kirchner: 6
    D. Pinkham
    K. Stockhausen: 10

c. $\frac{14}{8}$
  J. Barraqué: 1
  E. Carter: 4

d. $\frac{15}{8}$
  E. Carter: 3, 12
  P. Creston
  C. Debussy: 1, 7, 8
  P. Hindemith: 14, 16, 18
  C. Ives: 3
  E. Toch
  C. Wuorinen: 9

e. $\frac{16}{8}$
  G. Amy: 1
  W. Heider: 2
  H. Weisgall

f. $\frac{17}{8}$
  No examples located

g. $\frac{18}{8}$
  J. Alain: 2
  S. Barber: 6
  P. M. Davies: 4
  S. Prokofiev: 2
  O. Respighi

h. $\frac{19}{8}$
  J. Vincent

i. $\frac{20}{8}$
  W. Heider: 2
  S. Prokofiev
  I. Stravinsky: 17
  C. Wuorinen: 8

j. $\frac{21}{8}$
  J. Alain
  E. Carter: 11
  P. Creston
  P. M. Davies: 4
  W. Heider: 2
  C. Ives: 5
  E. Rubbra
  J. Schwantner
  K. Stockhausen: 10

k. $\frac{22}{8} - \frac{26}{8}$
  No examples located

l. $\frac{27}{8}$
  J. Gilboa

m. $\frac{28}{8} - \frac{32}{8}$
  No examples located

n. $\frac{33}{8}$
  J. Gilboa
  C. Ives: 5

o. $\frac{34}{8} - \frac{38}{8}$
  No examples located

p. $\frac{39}{8}$
  A. Hovhaness: 3

5. SIXTEENTH-NOTE DENOMINATORS.

a. $\frac{1}{16} - \frac{12}{16}$
  Examples too numerous to cite

b. $\frac{13}{16}$
  C. Ballif
  H. W. Henze: 2
  A. Hovhaness: 2
  C. Ives: 1

5. SIXTEENTH-NOTE DENOMINATORS—*continued.*

b. $\frac{13}{16}$

    L. Kirchner: 5, 7
    D. Martino: 2
    R. Sessions: 1

c. $\frac{14}{16}$

    C. Ballif
    J. Barraqué: 1
    E. Carter: 3, 4, 5, 7, 11, 12
    R. Harris: 1
    I. Stravinsky: 11

d. $\frac{15}{16}$

    Examples too numerous to cite

e. $\frac{16}{16}$

    G. Amy: 1
    T. Antoniou
    C. Ballif
    R. Harris: 1
    K. Stockhausen: 18

f. $\frac{17}{16}$

    C. Ballif
    R. Harris: 1
    A. Hovhaness: 2
    L. Janáček: 1

g. $\frac{18}{16}$

    E. Carter: 5, 11
    C. Ives: 1
    D. Martino: 2
    A. Schoenberg: 1
    R. Sessions: 2
    C. Wuorinen: 1

h. $\frac{19}{16}$

    C. Ballif
    L. Kirchner: 5

i. $\frac{20}{16}$

    C. Ballif
    E. Carter: 11
    R. Cordero

j. $\frac{21}{16}$

    E. Carter: 12
    D. Harris: 1
    C. Ives: 5

k. $\frac{22}{16}$

    No examples located

l. $\frac{23}{16}$

    C. Ballif

m. $\frac{24}{16}$

    C. Ballif
    E. Carter: 13

n. $\frac{25}{16}$

    D. Riley

o. $\frac{26}{16}-\frac{32}{16}$

    No examples located

p. $\frac{33}{16}$

    C. Ives: 5

6. THIRTY-SECOND-NOTE DENOMINATORS.

a. $\frac{1}{32}$

    G. Amy: 1
    P. Boulez: 2, 8
    W. Heider: 2
    C. Wuorinen: 2

b. $\frac{2}{32}$

    P. Boulez: 8
    N. Castiglioni
    K. Stockhausen: 18
    C. Wuorinen: 2

c. $\frac{3}{32}$

G. Amy: 1, 2
P. Boulez: 8
N. Castiglioni
D. Del Tredici: 1
K. Stockhausen: 5, 18
A. Webern: 3
C. Wuorinen: 2, 8

e. $\frac{5}{32}$

G. Amy: 2
P. Boulez: 8
M. Kagel: 1
P. Méfano: 1
D. Martino: 3
M. Powell: 2
K. Stockhausen: 18
C. Wuorinen: 1, 2, 5, 8

g. $\frac{7}{32}$

P. Boulez: 8
G. Crumb: 7, 9
Z. Durko: 1
H. W. Henze: 2
L. Kirchner: 4
D. Martino: 3
M. Powell: 2
K. Stockhausen: 18
C. Wuorinen: 2, 8

i. $\frac{9}{32}$

P. Boulez: 8
E. Carter: 5, 8, 11, 13
R. Helps: 1
D. Martino: 3
P. Méfano: 1
C. Nancarrow
M. Powell: 2
C. Wuorinen: 1, 6

k. $\frac{11}{32}$

D. Martino: 3
C. Nancarrow
C. Wuorinen: 2, 3, 5, 9

d. $\frac{4}{32}$

P. Boulez: 9
N. Castiglioni
D. Martino: 3
K. Stockhausen: 2
C. Wuorinen: 2

f. $\frac{6}{32}$

P. Boulez: 9
D. Martino: 3
C. Nancarrow
K. Stockhausen: 2, 3
C. Wuorinen: 2, 8

h. $\frac{8}{32}$

P. Boulez: 9
D. Martino: 3
K. Stockhausen: 2, 18

j. $\frac{10}{32}$

D. Martino: 3
C. Nancarrow
G. Rochberg: 2
C. Wuorinen: 5

l. $\frac{12}{32}$

G. Amy: 1
E. Carter: 11
P. Méfano: 1
C. Nancarrow
K. Stockhausen: 18
C. Wuorinen: 2, 8

6. THIRTY-SECOND-NOTE DENOMINATORS—*continued.*

m. $\frac{13}{32}$
T. Mayuzumi: 1
C. Nancarrow
C. Wuorinen: 1, 6

n. $\frac{14}{32}$
E. Carter: 5, 8, 10
G. Crumb: 8

o. $\frac{15}{32}$
G. Crumb: 9
C. Nancarrow
C. Wuorinen: 1, 3, 8

p. $\frac{16}{32}$
No examples located

q. $\frac{17}{32}$
T. Mayuzumi: 1

r. $\frac{18}{32}$
E. Carter: 5, 8
C. Nancarrow
C. Wuorinen: 1

s. $\frac{19}{32}$
No examples located

t. $\frac{20}{32}$
C. Nancarrow

u. $\frac{21}{32}$
E. Carter: 10
G. Crumb: 11

v. $\frac{22}{32}-\frac{23}{32}$
No examples located

w. $\frac{24}{32}$
E. Carter: 13

x. $\frac{25}{32}$
C. Nancarrow

y. $\frac{26}{32}-\frac{29}{32}$
No examples located

z. $\frac{30}{32}$
K. Stockhausen: 18
C. Wuorinen: 2

7. SIXTY-FOURTH-NOTE DENOMINATORS.

a. $\frac{1}{64}-\frac{4}{64}$
No examples located

b. $\frac{5}{64}$
C. Wuorinen: 1

c. $\frac{6}{64}$
No examples located

d. $\frac{7}{64}$
G. Crumb: 9
C. Wuorinen: 5

e. $\frac{8}{64}$
No examples located

f. $\frac{9}{64}$
C. Wuorinen: 5

g. $\frac{10}{64}$
No examples located

h. $\frac{11}{64}$
C. Wuorinen: 2

i. $\frac{12}{64}-\frac{14}{64}$
No examples located

j. $\frac{15}{64}$
C. Wuorinen: 5

k. $\frac{16}{64}-\frac{18}{64}$
No examples located

l. $\frac{19}{64}$
C. Wuorinen: 5

m. $\frac{20}{64}$
No examples located

n. $\frac{21}{64}$
G. Crumb: 7

Appendix B *Mixed Meters*

1. GREATER DENOMINATOR FIRST.

a. $\frac{1}{2} + \frac{1}{4}$
D. Martino: 1

b. $\frac{1}{2} + \frac{3}{8}$
D. Martino: 1

c. $\frac{1}{4} + \frac{1}{8}$
M. Babbitt: 3

d. $\frac{1}{4} + \frac{3}{8}$
M. Powell: 3
E. Varèse: 1

e. $\frac{1}{4} + \frac{1}{16}$
P. Boulez: 8

f. $\frac{1}{4} + \frac{2}{16}$
L. Nono

g. $\frac{1}{4} + \frac{3}{16}$
P. Boulez: 5
L. Nono

h. $\frac{1}{4} + \frac{5}{16}$
H. Birtwistle: 4
P. Boulez: 5
R. Haubenstock-
Ramati: 2

i. $\frac{1}{4} + \frac{1}{32}$
R. Helps: 2

j. $\frac{1}{8} + \frac{3}{16}$
P. Boulez: 5
P. Méfano: 2

k. $\frac{1}{8} + \frac{5}{16}$
G. Amy: 3

a. $\frac{2}{4} + \frac{1}{8}$
M. Babbitt: 3
J. Barraqué: 1
M. Davidovsky
D. Martino: 1

b. $\frac{2}{4} + \frac{3}{8}$
H. Birtwistle: 1
A. Copland: 8
P. M. Davies: 2
R. Haubenstock-
Ramati: 5
S. Matsushita: 4
B. Nilsson: 2
S. Revueltas
E. Varèse: 3

c. $\frac{2}{4} + \frac{5}{8}$
P. Boulez: 3
T. Mayuzumi: 1

d. $\frac{2}{4} + \frac{1}{16}$
W. Albright: 1

e. $\frac{2}{4} + \frac{3}{16}$
P. Boulez: 6, 9
H. W. Henze: 2
L. Kirchner: 3
M. Tippett: 2
C. Wuorinen: 8

f. $\frac{2}{4} + \frac{6}{16}$
L. Berio: 3
P. M. Davies: 2

g. $\frac{2}{8} + \frac{1}{16}$
P. Boulez: 6

h. $\frac{2}{8} + \frac{3}{16}$
M. Kagel: 2
P. Méfano: 2
M. Powell: 3

i. $\frac{2}{8} + \frac{5}{16}$
M. Kagel: 2

j. $\frac{2}{8} + \frac{6}{16}$
P. Boulez: 6

k. $\frac{2}{8} + \frac{1}{32}$
M. Powell: 1

l. $\frac{2}{8} + \frac{3}{32}$
H. W. Henze: 2
P. Méfano: 2
C. Wuorinen: 8

m. $\frac{2}{8} + \frac{5}{32}$
    M. Kagel: 2

n. $\frac{2}{16} + \frac{3}{32}$
    M. Kagel: 2
    P. Méfano: 2

a. $\frac{3}{2} + \frac{1}{4}$
    P. Boulez: 4
    Z. Kodály: 2

b. $\frac{3}{2} + \frac{3}{16}$
    P. Méfano: 2

c. $\frac{3}{4} + \frac{1}{8}$
    M. Babbitt: 3
    B. Bartók: 8
    M. Davidovsky
    M. Kagel: 1

d. $\frac{3}{4} + \frac{3}{8}$
    A. Copland: 8
    L. Kirchner: 3
    S. Matsushita: 1
    S. Revueltas
    G. Read: 2

e. $\frac{3}{4} + \frac{1}{16}$
    M. Kagel: 2
    R. Sessions: 1
    C. Wuorinen: 6

f. $\frac{3}{4} + \frac{1}{32}$
    C. Wuorinen: 8

g. $\frac{3}{4} + \frac{3}{32}$
    E. Carter: 13
    B. Nilsson: 1
    C. Wuorinen: 8

h. $\frac{3}{4} + \frac{5}{32}$
    C. Wuorinen: 8

i. $\frac{3}{8} + \frac{1}{16}$
    L. Berio: 2
    P. Boulez: 6
    N. Castiglioni
    M. Davidovsky

j. $\frac{3}{8} + \frac{3}{16}$
    P. Boulez: 9
    R. Haubenstock-
       Ramati: 5

k. $\frac{3}{8} + \frac{5}{16}$
    D. Harris: 2
    M. Kagel: 2

l. $\frac{3}{8} + \frac{1}{32}$
    C. Wuorinen: 8

m. $\frac{3}{8} + \frac{3}{32}$
    M. Kagel: 2
    C. Wuorinen: 8

n. $\frac{3}{8} + \frac{5}{32}$
    M. Kagel: 2

o. $\frac{3}{8} + \frac{12}{32}$
    E. Carter: 13

p. $\frac{3}{16} + \frac{3}{32}$
    M. Kagel: 2

a. $\frac{4}{4} + \frac{1}{8}$
    M. Babbitt: 3
    B. Bartolozzi
    M. Davidovsky
    L. Kirchner: 1
    T. Mayuzumi: 3
    R. Sessions: 1

b. $\frac{4}{4} + \frac{2}{8}$
    T. Mayuzumi: 3

c. $\frac{4}{4} + \frac{1}{32}$
    C. Wuorinen: 8

d. $\frac{4}{8} + \frac{1}{16}$
    P. Boulez: 6
    W. Lutoslawski

e. $\frac{4}{8} + \frac{3}{16}$
    H. W. Henze: 2
    M. Kagel: 2
    C. Wuorinen: 1

f. $\frac{4}{8} + \frac{1}{32}$
    M. Kagel: 2

g. $\frac{4}{8} + \frac{3}{32}$
    M. Kagel: 1
    C. Wuorinen: 8

h. $\frac{4}{8} + \frac{7}{32}$
    C. Wuorinen: 8

a. $\frac{5}{4} + \frac{1}{8}$
B. Bartolozzi
R. Sessions: 4

b. $\frac{5}{4} + \frac{1}{16}$
C. Wuorinen: 6

c. $\frac{5}{4} + \frac{3}{16}$
C. Wuorinen: 1

d. $\frac{5}{4} + \frac{7}{32}$
C. Wuorinen: 8

e. $\frac{5}{8} + \frac{1}{16}$
D. Riley
R. Sessions: 1

f. $\frac{5}{8} + \frac{3}{16}$
M. Kagel: 2
C. Wuorinen: 1

g. $\frac{5}{8} + \frac{5}{16}$
C. Wuorinen: 1

h. $\frac{5}{8} + \frac{1}{32}$
C. Wuorinen: 8

i. $\frac{5}{8} + \frac{3}{32}$
M. Kagel: 1

a. $\frac{6}{8} + \frac{1}{16}$
L. Berio: 2
H. Weisgall

b. $\frac{6}{8} + \frac{7}{32}$
C. Wuorinen: 1

2. LESSER DENOMINATOR FIRST.

a. $\frac{1}{4} + \frac{1}{2}$
D. Martino: 1

b. $\frac{1}{4} + \frac{2}{4}$
P. M. Davies: 2

c. $\frac{1}{8} + \frac{1}{4}$
I. Stravinsky: 18

d. $\frac{1}{8} + \frac{2}{4}$
R. Haubenstock-
Ramati: 5

e. $\frac{1}{8} + \frac{3}{4}$
B. Nilsson: 2
I. Stravinsky: 17

f. $\frac{1}{8} + \frac{4}{4}$
P. M. Davies: 2
B. Nilsson: 1

g. $\frac{1}{8} + \frac{6}{4}$
B. Nilsson: 1

h. $\frac{1}{16} + \frac{1}{4}$
P. Boulez: 9

i. $\frac{1}{16} + \frac{2}{4}$
A. Gilbert: 1

a. $\frac{3}{8} + \frac{1}{4}$
S. Matsushita: 1

b. $\frac{3}{8} + \frac{2}{4}$
A. Copland: 2
P. M. Davies: 2
S. Matsushita: 1
M. Tippett: 2

c. $\frac{3}{8} + \frac{3}{4}$
A. Copland: 2
L. Kirchner: 1

d. $\frac{3}{8} + \frac{4}{4}$
A. Copland: 2
L. Kirchner: 1

e. $\frac{3}{16} + \frac{1}{4}$
J. Barraqué: 3
P. Boulez: 6
R. Haubenstock-
Ramati: 5
P. Méfano: 2

f. $\frac{3}{16} + \frac{2}{4}$
A. Bancquart
R. Haubenstock-
Ramati: 5
C. Wuorinen: 1

g. $\frac{3}{16} + \frac{4}{4}$
P. Boulez: 6

h. $\frac{3}{16} + \frac{1}{8}$
P. M. Davies: 2

i. $\frac{3}{16} + \frac{2}{8}$
R. Haubenstock-
Ramati: 5
P. Méfano: 2

j. $\frac{3}{16} + \frac{3}{8}$
P. Boulez: 5
M. Kagel: 2

k. $\frac{3}{16} + \frac{4}{8}$
P. Boulez: 3

l. $\frac{3}{32} + \frac{1}{8}$
P. Méfano: 2

a. $\frac{5}{8} + \frac{1}{4}$
H. Birtwistle: 4

b. $\frac{5}{16} + \frac{1}{4}$
H. Birtwistle: 4
P. Boulez: 6

c. $\frac{5}{16} + \frac{2}{8}$
P. Boulez: 6
M. Kagel: 2

2. LESSER DENOMINATOR FIRST—*continued.*

a. $\frac{6}{16} + \frac{3}{2}$
G. Amy: 2

b. $\frac{6}{16} + \frac{2}{4}$
R. Haubenstock-
Ramati: 2

c. $\frac{6}{16} + \frac{3}{8}$
P. Boulez: 6
I. Stravinsky: 4

a. $\frac{9}{32} + \frac{3}{8}$
P. Méfano: 2

Appendix C   *Fractional Meters*

a. $\frac{2\frac{1}{2}}{2}$ ♩ ♩ ♩|
G. Read: 3

c. $\frac{1\frac{1}{4}}{4}$ ♩ ♪|
E. Varèse: 4

b. $\frac{6\frac{1}{2}}{2}$ ♩ ♩ ♩ ♩ ♩ ♩ ♩|
C. Ives: 16

d. $\frac{2\frac{1}{4}}{4}$ ♩ ♩ ♪|
C. Chávez: 2
I. Hamilton
Y. Irino: 2
M. Kupferman
T. Mayuzumi: 2
G. Read: 7
W. Riegger
D. Rudhyar
E. Varèse: 4

e. $\frac{3\frac{1}{4}}{4}$ ♩ ♩ ♩ ♪|
C. Chávez: 2
I. Hamilton
L. Harrison
M. Kupferman
T. Mayuzumi: 2
G. Read: 1
D. Rudhyar
F. Schmitt
K. Stockhausen: 5
E. Varèse: 2, 4, 5

f. $\frac{4\frac{1}{4}}{4}$ ♩ ♩ ♩ ♩ ♪|
C. Ives: 2
M. Kupferman
T. Mayuzumi: 2
G. Read: 1
D. Rudhyar
C. Wuorinen: 7

g. $\frac{5\frac{1}{4}}{4}$ ♩. ♩ ♪|
I. Hamilton
G. Read: 3

i. $\frac{10\frac{1}{4}}{4}$ ♩. ♩. ♩ ♩ ♪|
C. Wuorinen: 9

k. $\frac{2\frac{1}{2}}{8}$ ♫♩|
T. Takemitsu

h. $\frac{7\frac{1}{4}}{4}$ ♩. ♩ ♩ ♪|
C. Wuorinen: 6

j. $\frac{11\frac{1}{4}}{4}$ ♩. ♩. ♩. ♩ ♪|
C. Wuorinen: 6

l. $\frac{3\frac{1}{2}}{8}$ ♫♫♩|
G. Crumb: 5
T. Takemitsu

m. $\frac{4\frac{1}{2}}{8}$ ♫♫♫ |
C. Wuorinen: 9

n. $\frac{5\frac{1}{2}}{8}$ ♫♫♫♫ |
S. Revueltas
C. Wuorinen: 9

o. $\frac{9\frac{1}{2}}{8}$ ♩. ♩. ♩. ♫ |
C. Wuorinen: 9

p. $\frac{13\frac{1}{2}}{16}$ ♩. ♩. ♩. ♩. ♫ |
C. Wuorinen: 9

a. $\frac{3\frac{1}{2}}{4}$ ♩ ♩ ♩ ♫ |
H. Weinberg

b. $\frac{4\frac{3}{4}}{4}$ ♩ ♩ ♩ ♩ ♫♫ |
H. Weinberg

c. $\frac{20\frac{3}{4}}{8}$ ♩. ♩. ♩. ♩ ♫♫ |
C. Wuorinen: 2

a. $\frac{5\frac{1}{3}}{4}$
H. Weinberg

b. $\frac{1\frac{2}{3}}{4}$
D. Martino: 1

c. $\frac{2\frac{2}{3}}{4}$
H. Weinberg

d. $\frac{4\frac{2}{3}}{4}$
T. Mayuzumi: 2

e. $\frac{2\frac{4}{9}}{4}, \frac{3\frac{5}{9}}{4}$
H. Weinberg

f. $\frac{4\frac{1}{5}}{4}, \frac{2\frac{3}{5}}{4}, \frac{1\frac{3}{5}}{4}, \frac{4\frac{3}{5}}{4}, \frac{2\frac{1}{10}}{4}, \frac{3\frac{2}{10}}{4}, \frac{3\frac{1}{15}}{4}$
H. Weinberg

Appendix D   *Fractional Beats*

1. THIRDS, SIXTHS, NINTHS.

a. $\frac{1}{3}$ ♪♩♩
G. Amy: 2
S. Bussotti
J. Cage: 2
H. Cowell: 2, 4, 5
D. Martino: 2
B. Nilsson: 1
K. Stockhausen: 12
H. Weinberg
R. Wilding-White
C. Wolff: 1, 2

b. $\frac{2}{3}$ ♩♪♩
G. Amy: 2
P. Boulez: 5
J. Cage: 2
H. Cowell: 2, 4, 5
B. Nilsson: 1
K. Stockhausen: 12
H. Weinberg
R. Wilding-White
C. Wolff: 1, 2

c. $\frac{2}{3}$ ♩♩♩ (3:2)
P. Boulez: 5

d. $\frac{4}{3}$ ♩♩♩♩
J. Cage: 2
H. Cowell: 2
C. Wolff: 1, 2

1. THIRDS, SIXTHS, NINTHS—*continued*.

e. $\frac{5}{3}$ ⌐3⌐ (notation)

J. Cage: 2
H. Cowell: 2
C. Wolff: 1, 2

f. $\frac{1}{6}$ ⌐6:4⌐ (notation)

J. Cage: 2
H. Cowell: 5

g. $\frac{4}{6}$ ⌐6⌐ (notation)

H. Cowell: 4

h. $\frac{5}{6}$ ⌐6⌐ (notation)

H. Cowell: 4

i. $\frac{1}{9}$ 9:8 (notation)

H. Weinberg

j. $\frac{2}{9}$ ⌐9:8⌐ (notation)

D. Martino: 2

2. FIFTHS, TENTHS, FIFTEENTHS.

a. $\frac{1}{5}$ ⌐5:4⌐ (notation)

J. Cage: 2
H. Cowell: 2, 5
C. Nancarrow
H. Weinberg
C. Wolff: 1, 2

b. $\frac{2}{5}$ 5:4 (notation)

J. Cage: 2
H. Cowell: 2, 5
H. Weinberg
C. Wolff: 1, 2

c. $\frac{3}{5}$ ⌐5:4⌐ 7·[7] (notation)

J. Cage: 2
H. Cowell: 5
H. Weinberg
C. Wolff: 1, 2

d. $\frac{4}{5}$ ⌐5:4⌐ [7] (notation)

J. Cage: 2
H. Cowell: 5
H. Weinberg
C. Wolff: 1, 2

e. $\frac{1}{10}$ ⌐10:8⌐ (notation)

H. Weinberg

f. $\frac{1}{15}$ ⌐15:8⌐ (notation)

H. Cowell: 5
H. Weinberg

g. $\frac{2}{15}$ ⌐15⌐ (notation)

H. Cowell: 5

h. $\frac{4}{15}$ ⌐5⌐ (notation)

H. Cowell: 5

3. SEVENTHS.

J. Cage: 2

4. EIGHTHS.

In each case, the given fraction has been added to the ⬭ .

a, c, d: H. Cowell: 5   *b*: H. Weinberg

Bibliography

Bartolozzi, Bruno. "Proposals for Changes in Musical Notation." *Journal of Music Theory*, no. 5, 2 (1961): 297–301.

Blacher, Boris. "Über variable Metrik." Vienna: *Österreichische Musikzeitschrift*, nr. 6 (1962): 219–22.

Boulez, Pierre. *Boulez on Music Today*. Cambridge: Harvard University Press, 1971, pp.50–59, 97, 98, 135, 136.

Cooper, Grosvenor W., and Meyer, Leonard B. *The Rhythmic Structure of Music*. Chicago: University of Chicago Press, 1960.

Copland, Aaron. "On the Notation of Rhythm." *Modern Music*, no. 21, 4 (1944): 217–20.

Cowell, Henry. *New Musical Resources*. New York: Something Else Press, Inc., 1969.

Creston, Paul. *Principles of Rhythm*. New York: Franco Colombo, Inc., 1964.

Elston, Arnold. "Some Rhythmic Practices in Contemporary Music." *The Musical Quarterly*, no. 42, 3 (1956): 318–29.

Erickson, Robert. "Time-Relations." *Journal of Music Theory*, no. 7, 2 (1963): 174–92.

Friedheim, Philip. "Rhythmic Structure in Schoenberg's Atonal Compositions." *Journal of the American Musicological Society*, no. 19 (1966): 59–72.

Hindemith, Paul. *Elementary Training for Musicians*. New York: Associated Music Publishers, Inc., 1949.

Jones, Daniel. "Some Metrical Experiments." *The Score,* June 1950, pp.32–48.

Karkoschka, Erhard. *Notation in New Music: A Critical Guide to Interpretation and Realization*. Translated by Ruth Koenig. New York: Praeger Publishers, Inc., 1972.

Manziarly, Marcelle de. "On Rhythm, Complex and Simple." *Modern Music*, no. 21, 2 (1944): 70–75.

Messiaen, Olivier. *Technique of My Musical Language*. Translated by John Satterfield. Paris: Leduc et Cie., 1950.

Moore, Aubrey. "Improving Meter Notation." *The Instrumentalist*, no. 22, 4 (1967): 39.

Perkins, John M. "Note Values." *Perspectives of New Music*, no. 3, 2 (1965): 47–57.

Pike, Alfred. "The Time-Set as a Rhythmic Agent for the Series." *The Music Review*, no. 24, 2 (1963): 168–75.

Read, Gardner. *Music Notation: A Manual of Modern Practice*. 2d ed. Boston: Crescendo Publishing Co., 1971.

―――. "Some Problems of Rhythmic Notation." *Journal of Music Theory*, no. 9, 1 (1965): 153–62.

Riemann, Hugo. *System der musikalischen Rhythmik und Metrik*. Leipzig: Breitkopf & Härtel, 1903.

Sachs, Curt. *Rhythm and Tempo*. New York: W. W. Norton & Co., Inc., 1953.

Schillinger, Joseph. *Encyclopedia of Rhythms*. New York: Da Capo Press, Inc., 1976.

Smither, Howard E. "The Rhythmic Analysis of 20th-Century Music." *Journal of Music Theory*, no. 8, 1 (1964): 54–88.

―――, and Rzewski, Frederic. "Rhythm." *Dictionary of Contemporary Music*. Edited by John Vinton. New York: E. P. Dutton & Co., Inc., 1974, pp.618–22.

Weaver, H. E. "Syncopation: A Study of Musical Rhythms." *Journal of General Psychology*, no. 20 (1939): 409–29.

Winick, Steven D. *Rhythm: An Annotated Bibliography*. Metuchen (N.J.): The Scarecrow Press, Inc., 1974.

Wood, Ralph W. "The Rickety Bar." *Musical Times*, no. 45, 1338 (1954): 412–15.

Wuorinen, Charles. "Notes on the Performance of Contemporary Music." *Perspectives of New Music*, no. 3, 1 (1964): 10–21.

―――. "Performance." *Dictionary of Contemporary Music*. Edited by John Vinton. New York: E. P. Dutton & Co., Inc., 1974, pp.561–65.

Yeston, Maury. *The Stratification of Musical Rhythm*. New Haven: Yale University Press, 1975.

List of Publishers

AMPH	Amphion-Editions Musicales	JJ	Editions Jean Jobert
ARMP	Arrow Music Press, Inc.	KAL	Edwin F. Kalmus, Inc.
AVV	Ars Viva Verlag	LG	Lawson-Gould Music Publishers, Inc.
AMP	Associated Music Publishers, Inc.	LED	Leduc & Cie.
BAR	Bärenreiter-Verlag	LEED	Leeds Music Corporation
BDOL	Berandol Music Ltd.	LENG	Alfred Lengnick & Co., Ltd.
BMIC	BMI Canada, Ltd.	LIT	Henry Litolff's Verlag
BOM	Bomart Music Publications	MMX	McGinnis & Marx
BOON	Joseph Boonin, Inc.	MS.	Manuscript
BH	Boosey & Hawkes, Inc.	EBM	Edward B. Marks Music Corp.
B&B	Bote & Bock		
BR&H	Breitkopf & Härtel	MCA	MCA Music
AB	Alexander Broude, Inc.	MERC	Mercury Music Corporation
BRUZ	Edizioni Aldo Bruzzichelli	MIL	Mills Music, Inc.
CHAP	Chappell & Co., Ltd.	MJQ	M.J.Q. Music Co., Inc.
COLF	Colfranc Music Publishing Corp.	MV	Moeck-Verlag
		NME	New Musical Edition
DUR	Edition Durand	NOV	Novello & Company, Ltd.
EDM	Edito Musica	ONT	Ongaku-no-Tomo Sha, Inc.
EV	Elkan-Vogel, Inc.	OUP	Oxford University Press
ESCH	Editions Max Eschig	CFP	C. F. Peters Corporation
EUL	Ernst Eulenberg, Ltd.	PWM	Polskie Wydawnictwo Muzycne
CF	Carl Fischer, Inc.		
FOET	Foetisch Frères	TP	Theodore Presser Co.
GEN	General Music Publishing Co.	RIC	G. Ricordi & C.
		SAL	Editions Salabert
WH	Wilhelm Hansen Edition	ECS	E. C. Schirmer Music Co.
HEUG	Heugel & Cie.	GS	G. Schirmer, Inc.
HUD	Hudebni Matice Umelecke Besedy	SCHM	B. Schott's Söhne (Mainz)
		SCHL	Schott & Co., Ltd. (London)
IMP	Israeli Music Publications, Ltd.	SEE	Seesaw Music Corporation
		SEN	Edition Maurice Senart

SEP	Something-Else Press	STA	Stainer & Bell, Ltd.
SMP	Southern Music Publishing Co.	UE	Universal Edition, A.G.
		ZER	Edizioni Suvini Zerboni
SOV	Soviet State Music Publishers		

Index of Composers and Works